101 Things To Do With Rice

101 Things To Do With Rice

DONNA KELLY AND
STEPHANIE ASHCRAFT

GIBBS SMITH
TO ENRICH AND INSPIRE HUMANKIND

19 18 17 16 15   5 4 3 2 1

Text © 2015 Donna Kelly and Stephanie Ashcraft

101 Things is a registered trademark of Gibbs Smith, Publisher and Stephanie Ashcraft.

Published by
Gibbs Smith
P.O. Box 667
Layton, Utah 84041

1.800.835.4993 orders
www.gibbs-smith.com

Printed and bound in Korea
Gibbs Smith books are printed on either recycled, 100% post-consumer waste, FSC-certified papers or on paper produced from sustainable PEFC-certified forest/controlled wood source. Learn more at www.pefc.org.

Library of Congress Control Number: 2015936417

ISBN 13: 978-1-4236-4033-2

Dedication

This book is dedicated to the many people
who have loved, served, and inspired my
family. This includes family, friends, teachers,
neighbors, educators, and our church family.
We love you and appreciate you—S.A.

To all home cooks everywhere who serve
food with a side dish of love—Donna

Yum!
More recipes and tips
at 101yum.com

CONTENTS

Helpful Hints 9

Family Favorites

Sassy Sides and Salads

Savory Soups and Stews

Poultry and Seafood

Balsamic Chicken Stacks 64 • Cajun Chicken and Rice 65 • Salsa Chicken Bowl 66 • Chicken Green Chile Bake 67 • Tangy Chicken and Rice 68 • Bacon Ranch Chicken and Rice 69 • Hawaiian Haystacks 70 • Orange Rice and Orange Chicken 71 • Chicken Teriyaki Casserole 72 • Chicken Curry 73 • Chicken Stir-Fry 74 • Chicken Soft Tacos 75 • Asian Lettuce Wraps 76 • Mushroom and Artichoke Chicken 77 • Turkey Salad Croissants 78 • Shrimp Fried Rice 79 • Mango Mahi Mahi and Coconut Rice 80

Beef and Pork

Beef and Mushrooms 82 • Pineapple Meatballs and Rice 83 • Sweet and Sour Beef 84 • Hawaiian Fried Rice 85 • Hamburger Salsa Skillet 86 • Dinner Made Easy 87 • Broccoli Beef Stir-Fry 88 • Unstuffed Beef and Cabbage 89 • Aunt Leara's Zucchini Boats 90 • Bacon and Egg Fried Rice 91 • Slow Cooker Cajun Red Beans and Rice 92 • Pork Chop and Rice Bake 93

Around the World Entrees

Weeknight Skillet Paella (Spain) 96 • Arroz con Pollo (Puerto Rico) 97 • Bibimbap Bowl (Korea) 98 • Forbidden Rice (China) 99 • Pineapple Fried Rice (Thailand) 100 • Arancini Rice Balls (Sicily) 101 • Fragrant Stuffed Grape Leaves (Greece) 102 • Mujaddara Lentils and Rice (Middle East) 103 • Sushi Rice Bowls (Japan) 104 • Rice Stuffed Omelet Rolls (Japan) 105 • Burrito Rice Bowls (Mexico) 106 • Bolinhos de Arroz Fritters (Brazil) 107 • Canja Soup (Brazil) 108 • Chilean Rice (Chile) 109 • Plantains and Rice (Cuba) 110

Desserts and Sweet Treats

Chocolate Chip Rice Pudding 112 • Cherry Cheesecake Rice Pudding 113 • Classic Rice Pudding 114 • Cardamom Pistachio Rice Pudding 115 • Mango Sticky Rice 116 • Old Fashioned Baked Rice Custard 117 • Pumpkin Spice Rice Pudding 118 • Toffee Butterscotch Rice Pudding 119 • Dessert Sushi Rolls 120 • Hot Rice Cereal with Mango and Pineapple 121 • South of the Border Horchata 122

HELPFUL HINTS

1. To cook the perfect rice, keep lid on pan to prevent steam from escaping. Do not stir unless directed to do so in the recipe. Stirring will release starch causing rice to become sticky. At the end of specified cooking time, remove lid and test for doneness. If water has not been completely absorbed or rice is not tender, return to heat, cover and cook an additional 2−4 minutes, until done.

2. One cup uncooked rice equals 2 1/2−3 cups cooked rice. Two cups uncooked rice yields 5−6 cups cooked rice.

3. Many recipes in this cookbook call for cooked white rice. To cook traditional white rice: Use 1 cup of rice to 2 cups water or broth. Bring to a boil in a saucepan, reduce heat to low, cover and simmer for 15−20 minutes. Let stand, covered, for 5−10 minutes before serving. Three Step Perfect White Rice is wonderful in any recipe that calls for cooked white rice as well.

Three Step Perfect White Rice

2 cups	**long-grain white rice**
3 tablespoons	**vegetable oil**
4 cups	**hot water**
1 tablespoon	**lemon juice**
1 teaspoon	**salt**

In a medium saucepan over medium-high heat, cook the rice in the oil until most of the rice kernels turn opaque white, about 3 minutes, stirring frequently. Add water, lemon juice and salt. Turn heat to high and bring to a boil and stir rice. Reduce heat to low so that rice is simmering very slowly. Do not stir. Cover and cook 15−20 minutes, until all water is absorbed. Remove from heat, uncover and let stand for 5 minutes. Fluff with a fork.

4. To cook brown rice: Use 1 cup of rice to 2 cups of water or broth. Bring to a boil in a saucepan, reduce heat to low, cover and simmer for 45 minutes. Let stand, covered, for 5–10 minutes before serving.

5. To cook wild rice: Use 1 cup of rice to 3 cups of water or broth. Bring to a boil in a saucepan, reduce heat to low, cover and simmer for 45 minutes. Let stand, covered, for 5–10 minutes before serving.

6. Rice cookers simplify the cooking process and keep rice warm until ready to use. You can find ratios of rice to liquid, cooking time and amount yielded below.

1 Cup Uncooked Rice	Liquid	Cooking Time	Cooked Amount Yielded
Regular-milled long-grain	$1\frac{3}{4}$–2 cups	15 minutes	3–4 cups
Regular-milled medium-grain	$1\frac{1}{2}$ cups	15 minutes	3 cups
Regular-milled short-grain	$1\frac{1}{4}$ cups	15 minutes	3 cups
Whole grain brown	$2\frac{1}{4}$ cups	40–45 minutes	3–4 cups

7. The first time you try a recipe, check for doneness 5 minutes before its minimum cooking time is over. Each oven heats differently.

8. Low-fat, light, low-sugar or low-sodium ingredients can be substituted in any recipe. Ground turkey can be used in place of ground beef. Plain yogurt can be used in place of sour cream.

9. For more information on the different types of rice, visit the Whole Grains Council website, www.wholegrainscouncil.org/whole-grains-101/types-of-rice .

FAMILY
FAVORITES

SALMON RICE CAKES WITH RED PEPPER SAUCE

8 ounces	**uncooked salmon fillet***
1	**egg**
1/4 cup	**mayonnaise**
1/4 cup	**finely grated Parmesan cheese**
2 tablespoons	**minced shallot**
2 tablespoons	**minced fresh parsley**
1 cup	**cooked white rice**
1 cup	**panko-style breadcrumbs**
1 tablespoon	**oil or butter**
1 jar (12 ounces)	**roasted red peppers in oil**
2 tablespoons	**sour cream**
	salt and pepper, to taste

Cut salmon into 2 pieces and place in a single layer on a microwave-safe plate. Cook in microwave for approximately 3 minutes, or until salmon is cooked through and flakes easily. Let cool to room temperature and break into small pieces with a fork.

In a mixing bowl, whisk together the egg, mayonnaise, cheese, shallot and parsley. Stir in rice and salmon. Wet hands with water and form mixture into 4–6 small patties, about 2 inches thick. Spread breadcrumbs onto a plate. Press the patties into breadcrumbs, completely covering both sides. Refrigerate patties for at least 30 minutes.

In a frying pan over medium heat, add oil. Cook patties until they are cooked through and golden brown on each side. Place peppers in a blender. Add sour cream. Blend until smooth, adding a little liquid from the jar to thin the sauce as desired. Season with salt and pepper. Makes 2–4 servings.

* To save time, substitute with 1 can (8 ounces) salmon, drained and rinsed.

NEW ORLEANS JAMBALAYA

8 ounces	**andouille sausage**
1 tablespoon	**vegetable oil**
1/2	**onion,** minced
1/2	**red bell pepper,** diced
1 teaspoon	**Cajun seasoning**
3 cloves	**garlic,** minced
1 tablespoon	**tomato paste**
2 teaspoons	**cayenne pepper sauce**
2 cups	**cooked white rice**
1/2 cup	**vegetable broth**
16 ounces	**cooked peeled shrimp**
2 tablespoons	**minced fresh parsley**

Cut sausage in half lengthwise and then into 1/4 inch thick half-moon slices. Heat oil in a large frying pan to medium-high heat. Add sausage slices, onion, bell pepper and Cajun seasoning and saute for about 5 minutes, until vegetables are softened. Add garlic, tomato paste and cayenne pepper sauce; stir and cook for 1 minute. Stir in rice and broth and cover and simmer until rice has absorbed liquid, about 5 minutes. Remove from heat and stir in shrimp and parsley. Makes 4–6 servings.

GRANDMA'S STUFFED BELL PEPPERS

6	**green bell peppers**
1 pound	**ground beef or ground turkey**
1	**medium onion,** chopped
1 1/2 teaspoons	**minced garlic**
1 teaspoon	**Italian seasoning**
1 can (14.5 ounces)	**diced tomatoes with basil, garlic and oregano,** with liquid
3/4 cup	**uncooked instant white rice**
1 1/4 cups	**water,** divided
	salt and pepper, to taste
1 can (8 ounces)	**tomato sauce,** divided

Preheat oven to 350 degrees.

Bring a large pot of salted water to a boil. Cut the tops off the bell peppers and remove the seeds. Parboil the peppers in boiling water for 5 minutes. Carefully remove peppers and drain any excess water.

In a large frying pan, brown ground beef or turkey, onion and garlic until meat is no longer pink. Drain grease if necessary. Stir in the Italian seasoning, tomatoes, rice and 3/4 cup water. Cover, and simmer over medium heat for 5 minutes, or until rice is tender. Remove from heat. Season with salt and pepper.

Stuff each pepper with beef and rice mixture. Place stuffed peppers open side up in a baking dish. Place a spoonful of tomato sauce under each stuffed pepper using approximately 1/3 of the can. Spoon remaining tomato sauce over top of each stuffed pepper. Pour 1/2 cup water in bottom of baking dish. Cover with aluminum foil and bake 30 minutes, or until heated through. Makes 6 servings.

CRANBERRY RICE AND CHICKEN

I can (16 ounces)	**whole cranberry sauce**
I cup	**Russian salad dressing**
$1/4$ cup	**orange juice concentrate**
2–3 pounds	**boneless, skinless chicken breasts**
7 cups	**hot cooked rice**

In a small bowl, combine cranberry sauce, dressing and orange juice. Pour half the mixture into a 9 x 13-inch baking pan. Place chicken in pan in a single layer. Pour remaining sauce over chicken pieces. Cover and refrigerate at least 2 hours or overnight.

Preheat oven to 350 degrees.

Remove chicken from refrigerator, uncover and bring to room temperature, about 20 minutes. Bake for 60–70 minutes, basting occasionally. Serve over rice. Makes 6–8 servings.

CLASSIC CABBAGE ROLLS

1	**large cabbage,** halved
4 tablespoons	**butter or margarine**
1	**red onion,** diced
3 cloves	**garlic,** minced
2 stalks	**celery,** diced
1 tablespoon	**dried parsley**
1	**egg,** beaten
2 teaspoons	**salt**
1 teaspoon	**freshly ground black pepper**
2 cups	**cooked white rice**
1 1/2	**pounds ground beef**
2 cups	**chicken broth**
1 can (28 ounces)	**tomato puree**
2 tablespoons	**brown sugar**
2 tablespoons	**red wine vinegar**

Separate cabbage leaves and microwave a few at a time for about 90 seconds until soft and pliable. Melt butter in a large stock pot over medium heat and saute onion until soft. Add garlic and celery, saute for 1 minute. In a large mixing bowl, combine the onions, garlic, celery, parsley, egg, salt and pepper. Add the rice and ground beef, mixing well. In another bowl, combine broth, tomato puree, sugar and vinegar. Set aside.

In the center of each cooked cabbage leaf, place 1/4 cup of meat filling. Tuck in the sides of the leaf and starting with the stem end, roll the leaf tightly around filling. Place cabbage rolls in the stock pot, stacking neatly in layers. Cover rolls with tomato sauce mixture and bring to a boil. Cover tightly with a lid and simmer over low heat for 1 hour. Remove cabbage rolls to a serving plate leaving the remaining sauce. Turn up the heat to medium and simmer sauce mixture until reduced by half. Season with salt and pepper, to taste, and pour over rolls when ready to serve. Makes 6–8 servings.

STUFFED KALE ROLLS

2 tablespoons	**butter or margarine**
I teaspoon	**curry powder**
I cup	**uncooked long-grain white rice**
2 cups	**vegetable broth**
$^1/_4$ cup	**diced dried fruits,** such as apricots, cranberries or raisins
2 tablespoons	**diced walnuts, pecans or pistachios**
I tablespoon	**dried parsley**
2 ounces	**goat cheese,** crumbled
8	**large dinosaur kale leaves**
2 cups	**marinara sauce**

Preheat oven to 400 degrees.

Heat a large saucepan to medium-high heat. Add butter, curry powder and rice. Stir and cook until rice is translucent, about 3–5 minutes. Stir in vegetable broth. Reduce to a simmer and cover and cook for about 18–20 minutes, until liquid is no longer visible above the top of the rice. Uncover and cook another 3 minutes, letting liquid evaporate. Remove from heat and let stand 5 minutes. Fluff with a fork. Stir in fruits, nuts, parsley and goat cheese.

While rice is cooking, wash kale leaves and cut out most of core, leaving the very top of each leaf intact for rolling. Blanch the leaves in boiling water for I minute, or cook covered in a microwave oven until softened, about 90 seconds.

Place about $^1/_3$ cup of rice mixture at one end of each kale leaf and roll up. Spread some of the marinara in an 8 x 10-inch casserole dish. Place kale bundles in dish and pour remaining marinara over top. Cover with aluminum foil and bake for 25–30 minutes, until softened and bubbly. Serve immediately. Makes 4–6 servings.

PORCUPINE MEATBALLS

1 can (10.75 ounces)	**tomato soup,** condensed, divided
1 pound	**ground beef**
1 cup	**uncooked instant white rice**
1	**egg,** beaten
1/3 cup	**chopped onion**
1 teaspoon	**salt**
1/2 teaspoon	**pepper**
3/4 cup	**water**
1 teaspoon	**prepared mustard**
1 tablespoon	**minced garlic**

In a large bowl, combine 1/4 cup soup, ground beef, rice, egg, onion, salt and pepper. Shape into 16 meatballs.

In a large frying pan, brown meatballs about 7–10 minutes. Drain excess grease if necessary.

In a separate bowl, whisk together remaining soup, water, mustard and garlic. Pour mixture over meatballs. Cover and simmer over low heat 20 minutes, or until done, stirring occasionally. Makes 4 servings.

SUNDAY SUPPER CHICKEN AND RICE

4–6	**boneless, skinless chicken breasts**
2 cans (10.75 ounces each)	**cream of chicken soup,** condensed
1 package (1 ounce)	**dry onion soup mix**
1 cup	**sour cream or plain yogurt**
6 cups	**hot cooked rice**
	grated cheddar cheese, optional

Place chicken in a 3 1/2- to 5-quart slow cooker that has been prepared with nonstick cooking spray.

In a small bowl, combine canned soup and dry soup mix. Spread over chicken. Cover and cook on high heat 4 hours, or on low heat 6–8 hours. Thirty minutes before serving, stir sour cream into the chicken and sauce; shred the chicken using forks. Ladle chicken and sauce over individual servings of rice. Garnish with cheese if desired. Makes 4–6 servings.

SALSA CHICKEN

3–4	**boneless, skinless chicken breasts**
2 cups	**chunky salsa**
I can (10.75 ounces)	**cream of chicken soup,** condensed
6 cups	**hot cooked rice**
	grated cheddar cheese, optional

Place chicken in a 3- to 4½-quart slow cooker that has been prepared with nonstick cooking spray.

In a small bowl, combine salsa and soup. Spread soup mixture over chicken. Cover and cook on low heat for 6–8 hours. Shred chicken before serving. Ladle chicken and sauce over individual servings of rice. Garnish with cheese if desired. Makes 4–6 servings.

CREAMY SLOW COOKER CHICKEN

4	**boneless, skinless chicken breasts**
I envelope	**Italian salad dressing mix**
2 cans (10.75 ounces each)	**cream of chicken soup,** condensed
6 cups	**hot cooked rice**
	grated Italian blend cheeses, optional

Place chicken in a 3- to 4^1/2-quart slow cooker that has been prepared with nonstick cooking spray.

In a small bowl, combine dressing mix and soups. Spread soup mixture over chicken. Cover and cook on low heat for 6–8 hours. Cut chicken into chunks or shred before serving. Spoon sauce and chicken over individual servings of rice. Garnish with cheese, if desired. Makes 4–6 servings.

SWEET AND SOUR MEATBALLS

1	**egg,** beaten
1 cup	**seasoned breadcrumbs**
1 tablespoon	**minced garlic**
1/2 teaspoon	**salt**
1/4 teaspoon	**pepper**
2 pounds	**ground beef**
2 teaspoons	**olive oil**
1 cup	**chicken broth**
2	**large green bell peppers,** seeded and cut into chunks
2 cans (8 ounces each)	**unsweetened pineapple tidbits,** juice reserved
1/2 cup	**sugar**
3 tablespoons	**cornstarch**
1/2 cup	**apple cider vinegar**
2–3 tablespoons	**soy sauce**
8 cups	**hot cooked rice**

In a large bowl, combine egg, breadcrumbs, garlic, salt and pepper. Break up ground beef into egg mixture and combine well. Shape into 30–40 meatballs.

In a large frying pan, brown meatballs in oil for about 7-10 minutes. Add broth, bell peppers, and pineapple to meatballs. Bring to a boil. Reduce heat and simmer for 5–7 minutes.

In a separate bowl, combine sugar, cornstarch, vinegar, soy sauce and reserved pineapple juice until smooth. Pour over meatballs. Bring to a boil, reduce heat and simmer for 2 minutes, stirring constantly until thickened. Serve over rice. Makes 6–8 servings.

CHICKEN AND PARMESAN RICE

1 pound	**boneless, skinless chicken breasts,** cut into small pieces
1 tablespoon	**olive oil**
	salt and pepper, to taste
1 can (10.5 ounces)	**cream of chicken soup,** condensed
1 2/3 cups	**milk**
1/2 cup	**grated Parmesan cheese**
1/2 teaspoon	**Italian seasoning**
1	**large tomato,** diced
2 cups	**uncooked instant white rice**

In a large frying pan, saute chicken in hot oil until lightly browned. Season with salt and pepper.

While chicken cooks, combine soup, milk, cheese and seasoning in a large saucepan. Heat until it starts to bubble. Stir in tomato and instant rice. Cover and cook over low heat for 5 minutes, or until rice is done. Serve chicken over individual servings of rice. Makes 4 servings.

SUMMER ZUCCHINI TOMATO CASSEROLE

1/3 cup	**uncooked long-grain white rice**
2/3 cup	**water**
4 cups	**cubed zucchini**
2/3 cup	**diced red onion**
1 tablespoon	**minced garlic**
2 tablespoons	**olive oil**
1 teaspoon	**salt**
1 1/2 teaspoons	**Italian seasoning**
1 teaspoon	**paprika**
1 1/2 cups	**seeded, chopped tomatoes**
1 1/2 cups	**grated sharp cheddar cheese,** divided

In a medium saucepan, combine rice and water. Bring to a boil. Cover and reduce heat to low. Simmer 20 minutes, or until rice is done.

Preheat oven to 350 degrees.

In a large frying pan over medium heat, saute zucchini, onion and garlic in olive oil for 5 minutes, until tender. Add the salt, Italian seasoning and paprika. Stir in cooked rice, tomatoes, and 1 cup cheese. Spoon zucchini mixture into a 1 1/2-quart casserole dish prepared with nonstick cooking spray. Sprinkle remaining cheese evenly over top. Bake uncovered for 20 minutes. Makes 6 servings.

CHICKEN AND BROCCOLI CASSEROLE

I pound	**broccoli,** cut into small florets
$^1/_3$ cup	**flour**
3	**eggs**
$^1/_2$ cup	**sour cream**
I cup	**milk**
I tablespoon	**Dijon mustard**
4 ounces	**grated cheddar cheese,** divided
2 cups	**cooked white rice**
2 cups	**I-inch cubed, cooked chicken**

Preheat oven to 350 degrees.

Place broccoli pieces on a microwave-safe plate and microwave for about 2 minutes, or until just fork tender. Set aside.

In a medium bowl, whisk together the flour and eggs. Add the sour cream, milk, mustard and half of the cheese; stir to combine.

Prepare a 9 x 13-inch baking pan with nonstick cooking spray. Spread rice into bottom of pan. Pour egg mixture over rice and top with broccoli pieces and chicken. Sprinkle with remaining cheese. Bake for 20–25 minutes, or until cheese is lightly browned. Makes 4–6 servings.

BAKED ASPARAGUS
RISOTTO PRIMAVERA

I can (10.75 ounces)	**cream of asparagus soup,** condensed
1 1/2 cups	**water**
I can (12 ounces)	**evaporated milk**
1/4 cup	**grated Parmesan cheese**
I teaspoon	**salt**
I cup	**diced asparagus**
1/2 cup	**diced bell pepper,** any color
I cup	**uncooked risotto rice***
2 tablespoons	**dried basil or parsley**

Preheat oven to 400 degrees.

In a large bowl, stir together all ingredients. Pour into a 2 1/2-quart casserole dish. Cover and bake 30 minutes; uncover and stir. Bake uncovered another 10 minutes. Remove from oven and let stand 10 minutes before serving. Garnish with additional parsley or basil flakes, if desired. Makes 6–8 servings as a side dish.

*Do not rinse risotto before using in recipe. This will destroy the starch, and risotto will not be creamy.

Garlic Mushroom Variation: Replace asparagus soup with cream of mushroom and roasted garlic soup. Replace asparagus with diced button mushrooms. Replace bell peppers with diced yellow onions.

CHICKEN FIESTA CASSEROLE

2 tablespoons	**vegetable oil**
1/2	**onion,** diced
1/2	**green bell pepper,** diced
1 tablespoon	**chili powder**
2 teaspoons	**cumin**
1 teaspoon	**salt**
1 tablespoon	**brown sugar**
3 cups	**cooked white rice**
1/2 cup	**favorite medium or hot salsa,** any style
1/2 cup	**sour cream**
1 can (15 ounces)	**black beans,** drained
1 cup	**fresh or frozen corn**
2 cups	**1-inch cubed, cooked chicken breast**
4 ounces	**grated sharp cheddar cheese**

Preheat oven to 350 degrees.

In a large frying pan, heat oil over medium-high heat; add onions and bell pepper and saute until vegetables are fork tender. Stir in chili powder, cumin, salt and sugar and cook for 1 minute. Stir in rice, salsa, sour cream, beans and corn.

Spread mixture into a 9 x 13-inch pan that has been prepared with nonstick cooking spray. Sprinkle the chicken and cheese over top. Bake at top of oven for 25–30 minutes, until cooked through and lightly browned. Serve with optional garnishes, such as salsa, sour cream, diced tomatoes, diced green onions and diced cilantro. Makes 6–8 servings.

SASSY SIDES AND SALADS

SPRING CELEBRATION RICE

3 cups	**water**
1 teaspoon	**salt**
1 tablespoon	**butter or vegetable oil**
1 tablespoon	**lemon juice**
1 1/2 cups	**uncooked long-grain white rice**
1 cup	**frozen petite peas,** thawed
1/4 cup	**minced dill leaves**
1 teaspoon	**lemon zest**

In a large saucepan, bring the water, salt, butter and lemon juice to a boil. Add rice. Bring to a boil and reduce to a simmer. Cover and cook for 20 minutes, or until all liquid is absorbed. Remove from heat and let sit uncovered for 5 minutes. Add peas, dill and zest; fluff with a fork. Makes 4–6 servings.

KITCHEN SINK RICE

2 tablespoons	**vegetable oil**
$1/2$ cup	**diced onion**
$1/2$ cup	**diced green bell pepper**
$1/2$ cup	**diced celery**
1 teaspoon	**turmeric**
1 can (15 ounces)	**diced tomatoes,** with liquid
1 cup	**chicken broth**
1 teaspoon	**cayenne pepper sauce**
1 cup	**uncooked long-grain white rice**
8 ounces	**ham,** cut in $1/4$-inch cubes
1 cup	**frozen diced peas and carrots,** thawed

In a large saucepan, heat the oil on medium-high heat. Add onion, bell pepper and celery and cook until softened, about 3–5 minutes. Add turmeric and cook for 1 minute.

Stir in tomatoes, broth, pepper sauce and rice. Bring to a boil and reduce to a simmer. Cover and cook 20 minutes, until liquid is absorbed. Stir in ham and peas and carrots. Makes 4–6 servings.

LOUISIANA DIRTY RICE

1 1/2 cups	**uncooked long-grain white rice**
3 cups	**chicken broth**
3 slices	**bacon,** diced
8 ounces	**andouille sausage,** cut in 1/4-inch slices
4 ounces	**chopped chicken livers**
1/2	**onion,** finely diced
2 stalks	**celery,** finely diced
1/2	**green bell pepper,** finely diced
1 tablespoon	**Cajun seasoning**
1 tablespoon	**cayenne pepper sauce**
2	**green onions,** thinly sliced

In a large saucepan, bring the rice and chicken broth to a boil, reduce heat, cover and simmer until all liquid is absorbed, about 20 minutes. Spread the rice on a baking sheet and cool.

Cook the bacon in a large frying pan until crispy. Remove bacon and let drain on a paper towel, leaving fat in the pan. Add the sausage and chicken livers to same frying pan and saute until cooked through. Place the bacon, sausage and livers in a food processor and pulse a few times until very small bits.

Cook the onion, celery and bell pepper in the same frying pan until very soft and lightly browned. Stir the rice and the meat mixture into the onions. Stir in the seasoning, pepper sauce and green onions. Makes 6–8 servings as a side dish.

NEW YEAR'S HOPPIN' JOHN RISOTTO

1 quart	**vegetable broth**
3 tablespoons	**butter or vegetable oil**
1	**large yellow onion,** diced
2 cloves	**garlic,** minced
1 1/2 cups	**uncooked Arborio rice**
1/3 cup	**white wine**
4 cups	**chopped spinach**
juice and zest of 1	**lemon**
1/2 teaspoon	**thyme**
1 can (15 ounces)	**black-eyed peas,** drained and rinsed
1/2 cup	**grated Parmesan cheese,** optional
	salt and pepper, to taste

Heat the broth in a large saucepan at the back of the stovetop and keep it at a low simmer.

In a large frying pan over medium-high heat, melt the butter and add the onion. Saute for 3–4 minutes, until onion starts to soften. Stir in the garlic and rice making sure rice is completely coated with melted butter. Add the wine and stir until evaporated. Begin adding in the broth, one ladle at a time, stirring after every addition. Let the rice simmer after adding each ladle-full of broth, until most of the liquid is absorbed, before adding another ladle of broth.

Once you get down to the last few ladles of broth, start checking the bite of the rice. When it is nearly done, add the spinach to the broth that's left in the pot and let it cook down a bit. Add the lemon juice, zest and thyme to the rice. Add the remaining broth and greens to the pot, and then gently stir in the black-eyed peas. Remove from heat, add the cheese and season with salt and pepper. Makes 6–8 servings.

GREEN GOODESS RICE

1 ½ cups	**uncooked long-grain white rice**
3 cups	**low sodium vegetable broth**
1	**large ripe Haas avocado,** peeled and pit removed
2 tablespoons	**lime juice**
1 teaspoon	**lime zest**
1 cup	**chopped fresh parsley**
¼ cup	**olive oil**
1 teaspoon	**cayenne pepper sauce**
	salt and pepper, to taste

In a large saucepan, bring rice and broth to a boil. Reduce heat, cover and simmer for 18–20 minutes, until all liquid is absorbed and rice is tender. Remove from heat and let stand 5 minutes.

In blender, blend avocado, lime juice, zest, parsley, olive oil and pepper sauce until smooth, adding a little water if needed to make the consistency of sour cream. Stir avocado mixture into rice and season with salt and pepper. Serve warm. Makes 6–8 servings.

SPANISH RICE

1/4 cup	**chopped onion**
2 tablespoons	**olive oil**
1 1/2 cups	**uncooked long-grain white rice**
1/2 cup	**water**
2 cups	**chicken broth**
1 cup	**chunky salsa**
1/4 teaspoon	**chili powder**

In a large frying pan, saute onion in hot oil until translucent. Stir rice into frying pan coating the rice with oil and onions. Stir in water, broth, salsa and chili powder. Bring to a boil. Reduce heat to low, cover and simmer for 15–20 minutes, until rice is done. Makes 5–6 servings.

CLASSIC RICE PILAF

3 tablespoons	**butter or margarine**
$^1/_4$ cup	**minced onion**
1 cup	**uncooked basmati rice**
2 cups	**water**
1 teaspoon	**salt**
$^1/_2$ cup	**finely diced toasted nuts, dried fruits, minced fresh herbs,** or any combination of these, optional

In a medium saucepan over medium-high heat, melt the butter and saute the onion until translucent, about 3–5 minutes. Stir the rice into the pan and cook until most of the rice has turned opaque white.

Stir in water and salt and bring to a boil. Reduce heat to low, cover and cook at a slow simmer until all water is absorbed, 15–18 minutes. Do not stir. Remove from heat. Remove lid and place a kitchen towel over pan. Put lid back on over towel and let sit for 10 minutes. Remove lid and towel and fluff the rice with a fork. Add nuts, fruits or herbs as desired. Makes 4–6 servings.

BAKED MUSHROOM RICE

2 tablespoons	**butter or margarine**
$^1/_2$ cup	**diced onion**
3 cups	**thinly sliced mushrooms***
3 cups	**vegetable broth**
$^1/_2$ cup	**apple juice**
I tablespoon	**apple cider vinegar**
2 cups	**uncooked long-grain white rice**
$^1/_2$ cup	**sour cream**
	salt and pepper, to taste

Preheat oven to 375 degrees.

Melt butter in a large frying pan over medium-high heat. Add onion and cook until translucent, about 3 minutes. Add mushrooms and cook until tender. Stir remaining ingredients into pan and cook about 3 minutes, until mixture is heated through.

Prepare a 9 x 13-inch baking pan with nonstick cooking spray. Pour in the rice mixture, cover with aluminum foil and bake for 50–60 minutes, or until liquid is absorbed. Taste and season with salt and pepper as desired. Makes 6–8 servings.

* Use any combination of mushrooms you like, such as cremini, shiitake caps, white button mushrooms or oyster mushrooms.

FRENCH ONION MUSHROOM RICE

1 cup	**uncooked long-grain white rice**
¹/₄ cup	**butter or margarine,** melted
1 can (10.5 ounces)	**French onion soup,** condensed
1 can (10.5 ounces)	**beef broth**
1 teaspoon	**minced garlic**
1 can (4 ounces)	**sliced mushrooms,** drained

Preheat oven to 350 degrees.

In a medium bowl, combine rice and butter. Stir in soup, broth, garlic and mushrooms. Spread rice mixture into an 8 x 8-inch pan that has been prepared with nonstick cooking spray. Cover with aluminum foil and bake for 60 minutes. Makes 4 servings.

SLOW COOKER BLACK BEANS AND RICE

2 cans (15 ounces each)	**black beans,** drained and rinsed
1 1/2 cups	**water**
3/4 cup	**salsa**
3/4 cup	**uncooked long-grain white rice**
1 1/2 teaspoons	**cumin**
1 teaspoon	**chili powder**
1 teaspoon	**garlic powder**
1/2 teaspoon	**salt**
1/2 teaspoon	**black pepper**

Prepare the inside of a 3-quart slow cooker with nonstick cooking spray. Add all the ingredients to the slow cooker and gently stir. Cover and cook on low for 3 hours. Serve as a side, a filling for tortillas or over tortilla chips with shredded cheese sprinkled over top. Makes 4–6 servings.

PARMESAN RICE

4 tablespoons	**butter or margarine**
1 tablespoon	**minced garlic**
1 cup	**uncooked long-grain white rice**
1 cup	**water**
1 cup	**low-fat milk**
$1/2$ teaspoon	**salt**
$1/2$ cup	**grated Parmesan cheese**
$1/2$ tablespoon	**chopped fresh parsley,** optional
	salt and pepper, to taste

In a medium saucepan, melt butter. Add garlic and saute for 3 minutes. Stir rice into butter to coat. Add water, milk and salt; stir and bring to a boil. Reduce heat to low, cover pan and cook for 20 minutes until rice is done, stirring occasionally to prevent rice from sticking to bottom of pan.

Remove from heat and stir in cheese and parsley, if using. Season with salt and pepper. Cover and let stand for 5 minutes before serving. Makes 2–3 servings.

WILD RICE MIX CASSEROLE

1 cup	**wild rice and grains mix**
$^1/_2$	**red bell pepper,** diced
3	**green onions,** thinly sliced
2 tablespoons	**minced fresh parsley**
3	**eggs,** beaten
$^1/_2$ cup	**sour cream**
1 ounce	**grated Parmesan cheese,** divided

Preheat oven to 350 degrees.

Cook wild rice mix according to package directions. Remove from heat and let cool to warm.

In a medium bowl, mix together the bell pepper, onions, parsley, eggs, sour cream and half of the cheese. Stir this mixture into the cooked rice.

Prepare a 2-quart casserole dish with nonstick cooking spray. Spoon in the rice mixture and top with remaining cheese. Bake for 25–30 minutes, until browned. Makes 4–6 servings.

CRANBERRY PECAN WILD RICE SALAD

I cup	**brown and wild rice mix***
2 1/3 cups	**water**
1/2 teaspoon	**salt**
I tablespoon	**butter or margarine**
3/4 cup	**dried cranberries**
3/4 cup	**chopped pecans**
1/4 cup	**sliced green onions**
I tablespoon	**sugar or sugar substitute**
1/2 teaspoon	**dried minced onion**
1/2 teaspoon	**poppy seeds**
1/8 teaspoon	**paprika**
2 tablespoons	**apple cider vinegar**
2 tablespoons	**olive oil**

In a large saucepan, bring rice mix, water, salt and butter to a boil. Reduce heat to low, cover and simmer for 45–50 minutes. Remove rice from heat and cool covered for 10 minutes. Remove lid and fluff rice with a fork. Fold in cranberries, pecans and green onions.

In a small bowl, whisk together sugar, minced onion, poppy seeds, paprika, vinegar and olive oil. Just before serving, mix dressing into the rice mixture. Serve warm, chilled or at room temperature. Makes 4–6 servings.

*Usually found in bulk bins at larger grocery stores. If not available, brown rice can be used with only 2 cups water. Salt and butter amounts remain the same.

WILD RICE
AVOCADO CHICKEN SALAD

2 1/2 cups	**water**
I cup	**uncooked wild rice**
4 tablespoons	**lemon juice**
2 cups	**cubed, cooked chicken**
I	**red bell pepper,** diced
I 1/2 cups	**sugar snap peas,** cut into pieces
I cup	**chopped pecan halves**
2	**avocados,** cubed

Dressing:

2 teaspoons	**minced garlic**
I tablespoon	**Dijon mustard**
1/2 teaspoon	**salt**
1/4 teaspoon	**pepper**
1/4 cup	**sugar**
1/4 cup	**apple cider vinegar**
1/3 cup	**olive oil**

In a medium saucepan, bring water to a boil. Stir in wild rice. Reduce heat and simmer, covered 40–45 minutes, or just until kernels puff open. Remove lid, fluff with a fork and simmer an additional 5 minutes. Rinse cooked rice in cold water and drain thoroughly.

In a large bowl, toss rinsed rice with lemon juice. Allow rice to cool completely. Stir in the chicken, bell pepper, peas and pecans.

Whisk together the dressing ingredients in a separate bowl. Add dressing to the salad mixture and toss to coat. Mix in cubed avocado right before serving. Serve at room temperature or chilled. Makes 6–8 servings.

CHICKEN AND RICE SALAD

2	**boneless, skinless chicken breasts,** cooked and finely diced
3 cups	**cooked rice**
1 cup	**frozen peas,** thawed
1 cup	**diced celery**
$^1/_2$	**red bell pepper,** diced
1 cup	**toasted sliced almonds**
3	**green onions,** thinly sliced
1 can (8 ounces)	**pineapple tidbits,** with juice
1 cup	**Italian dressing**
$^1/_2$ cup	**toasted sesame seeds,** divided

Combine all ingredients except dressing and sesame seeds in a medium-size serving bowl. Refrigerate 2 hours or overnight. Toss with dressing and $^1/_4$ cup sesame seeds before serving. Sprinkle remaining sesame seeds over top as a garnish. Makes 8–10 servings.

MARDI GRAS SALAD

1 1/3 cups	**water**
2/3 cup	**uncooked long-grain white rice**
1/3 cup	**real crumbled bacon**
1/2 cup	**frozen tiny salad shrimp**
1/2 cup	**cubed andouille sausage or ham**
1/2 cup	**sliced celery**
1/4 cup	**chopped onion**
1/2 cup	**chopped red bell pepper**
1 cup	**chopped tomato**
3/4 cup	**Italian salad dressing**
1 teaspoon	**dried thyme**
1/4 teaspoon	**chili powder**
1 teaspoon	**minced garlic**
1/4 teaspoon	**Cajun seasoning**

In a medium saucepan, bring water to a boil before stirring in the rice. Cover, reduce heat to low and simmer 20 minutes until rice is done.

In a large bowl, combine the cooked rice, crumbled bacon, shrimp, sausage or ham, celery, onion, bell pepper and tomatoes.

In a separate bowl, whisk together the Italian salad dressing, thyme, chili powder, minced garlic and seasoning. Pour dressing over rice mixture; toss to coat. Refrigerate for 3 hours or overnight before serving. Makes 4–6 servings.

HAWAIIAN HAYSTACK SALAD

³/₄ cup	**mayonnaise**
3 tablespoons	**apple cider vinegar**
2 tablespoons	**olive oil**
2¹/₂ cups	**cubed, cooked chicken**
2 cups	**cooked rice**
¹/₂ cup	**dried cranberries or diced dried cherries**
1 cup	**chopped celery**
1 can (11 ounces)	**mandarin oranges,** drained
1 can (8 ounces)	**pineapple tidbits,** drained
¹/₃ cup	**chopped green onion**
	salted peanuts or cashews, for garnish
	chow mein noodles, for garnish

In a large bowl, mix together the mayonnaise, vinegar and olive oil until smooth. Fold in the chicken, rice, cranberries, celery, oranges, pineapple and green onion until evenly coated. Cover and refrigerate for at least 3 hours or overnight. Garnish individual servings with nuts and chow mein noodles immediately before serving. Makes 8–10 servings.

CHEESY ZUCCHINI RICE

I tablespoon	**vegetable oil**
I cup	**uncooked long-grain white rice**
2 cups	**vegetable broth**
I	**medium zucchini,** unpeeled
I tablespoon	**butter or vegetable oil**
I cup	**grated sharp cheddar cheese**
I teaspoon	**garlic powder**
	salt and pepper, to taste

Heat the olive oil in a large saucepan over medium-high heat. Add rice and stir, cooking until rice turns golden. Pour in the broth and bring to a boil. Turn heat to low, cover and cook for 20 minutes, or until liquid is absorbed.

Grate the zucchini using the large holes of a box grater over a clean kitchen towel. Hold the towel with zucchini in the middle over the sink and squeeze until most of liquid is removed.

While rice is still very hot, add the zucchini, butter, cheese and garlic powder and stir until cheese is melted. Season with salt and pepper. Makes 4–6 servings.

COWBOY RICE

1 strip	**beef jerky,** about 1 inch wide and 4 inches long
1 can (15 ounces)	**hominy,** drained and rinsed
1 can (15 ounces)	**black-eyed peas,** drained and rinsed
1 can (15 ounces)	**black beans,** drained and rinsed
1	**small ripe tomato,** diced
2	**green onions,** thinly sliced
2 cups	**cooked rice,** any variety, chilled
2 tablespoons	**extra-virgin olive oil**
1 tablespoon	**red wine vinegar**
$^1/_4$ teaspoon	**salt**
1 teaspoon	**cayenne pepper sauce**
2 tablespoons	**chopped, fresh cilantro**

Pour boiling water over beef jerky and let sit at room temperature for about 30 minutes, until softened. Drain water off and mince.

In a large bowl, stir together the minced beef jerky, hominy, black-eyed peas, black beans, tomato, green onions and rice.

In a small bowl, whisk together the olive oil, vinegar, salt, pepper sauce and cilantro. Toss into rice mixture. Serve chilled or at room temperature. Makes 6 –8 servings.

SAVORY RICE SOUFFLE

6	**eggs,** separated
1/2 teaspoon	**cream of tartar**
I cup	**whipping cream**
2 ounces	**grated Swiss or Gruyere cheese**
2 cups	**cooked white rice**
I teaspoon	**salt**
1/4 teaspoon	**white pepper**
4 slices	**cooked bacon,** minced
3	**green onions,** thinly sliced

Preheat oven to 350 degrees.

In a medium bowl, beat the egg whites and cream of tartar together until stiff peaks form. Set aside.

In a small bowl, beat the egg yolks into the cream. Stir in the cheese, rice, salt, pepper, bacon and onions. Carefully fold in the beaten egg whites and pour into a buttered 2-quart souffle dish. Bake for 45–50 minutes, until souffle is set in center. Makes 4–6 servings.

SAVORY SOUPS AND STEWS

CREAMY CHICKEN AND RICE SOUP

3 tablespoons	**unsalted butter or margarine**
I cup	**diced carrots**
I cup	**diced onion**
I cup	**diced celery**
$1/4$ cup	**chopped fresh parsley**
$1/2$ teaspoon	**freshly ground black pepper**
I teaspoon	**dried thyme leaves**
$1/2$ teaspoon	**garlic powder**
$1/4$ cup	**flour**
4 cups	**low sodium chicken broth**
2 cups	**cubed, cooked chicken**
I cup	**uncooked instant white rice**
I cup	**frozen green peas**
I cup	**heavy cream**
	salt and pepper, to taste

In a large pot over medium-high heat, melt butter and add carrots, onion, celery, parsley, pepper, thyme and garlic powder. Stir and cook for 5 minutes. Lower heat to medium and add flour. Stir and cook for 3 more minutes. Add broth and stir until combined. Add chicken and rice and stir. Reduce heat to low and simmer for about 10 minutes, until rice and vegetables are softened.

When rice is almost done, add peas and cream; stir and cook for about 2 more minutes. Season with salt and pepper. Makes 4–6 servings.

LEMON ARTICHOKE RICE SOUP

2 tablespoons	**coconut oil**
1 cup	**uncooked long-grain white rice**
1	**onion,** diced
2 stalks	**celery,** diced
1	**carrot,** peeled and diced
1 quart	**chicken or vegetable broth**
1 cup	**water**
1 jar (8 ounces)	**artichoke hearts,** drained and diced
juice and zest of 1	**large lemon**
1 teaspoon	**salt**
$^1/_2$ teaspoon	**pepper**
$^1/_2$ cup	**diced fresh parsley,** plus extra for garnish
$^1/_4$ cup	**diced fresh chives**

Heat the oil in a large stock pot over medium-high heat. Add the rice and saute until opaque, about 3 minutes. Add the onion, celery and carrot and cook until softened. Add the broth, water, artichoke hearts, lemon juice, zest, salt and pepper. Bring to a boil, reduce heat and simmer for about 20 minutes.

Ladle 1 cup of soup into a blender and blend until smooth. Pour back into pot and stir. Add parsley and chives. Garnish with extra parsley when ready to serve. Makes 4–6 servings.

GOOD TIMES ROLL GUMBO

¹/₂ cup	**peanut or canola oil,** divided
3	**skinless bone-in chicken thighs**
¹/₂ cup	**flour**
1	**medium yellow onion,** diced
1	**green bell pepper,** diced
1 stalk	**celery,** diced
6 cups	**chicken broth**
4 ounces	**andouille sausage,** or other spicy smoked sausage
1 cup	**fresh or frozen okra,** sliced into ¹/₂-inch chunks
1 tablespoon	**Worcestershire sauce**
1 tablespoon	**file gumbo powder**
1 tablespoon	**smoked paprika**
1 tablespoon	**honey**
1 tablespoon	**Louisiana hot sauce,** or cayenne pepper sauce
2 tablespoons	**apple cider vinegar**
	salt and pepper, to taste
3 cups	**cooked white rice**

In a large pot, over medium-high heat add 3 tablespoons of oil. Add chicken and saute about 4 minutes per side, until golden brown. Remove chicken and set aside. Pour remaining oil into pan. Slowly whisk in flour. Reduce heat to medium-low and simmer for about 10–12 minutes, whisking frequently until roux is a medium brown. Stir in onions and cook for another 15–20 minutes, stirring frequently. Add bell pepper and celery. Slowly whisk in the broth. Return chicken to the pot. Turn heat to low, cover and simmer for 1 hour, stirring occasionally. Add sausage, okra, Worcestershire sauce, file, paprika, honey and hot sauce. Cover and simmer for 1 more hour, stirring occasionally. Remove from heat, add vinegar and season with salt and pepper. Serve over rice. Makes 6–8 servings.

ITALIAN WEDDING SOUP

8 ounces	**uncooked mild sweet Italian sausage,** without casings
$1/3$ cup	**dried breadcrumbs**
2 tablespoons	**finely grated Parmesan cheese**
I	**egg,** beaten
2 tablespoons	**vegetable oil**
I	**carrot,** peeled and diced
I stalk	**celery,** diced
$1/2$	**onion,** diced
3 cloves	**garlic,** minced
6 cups	**chicken broth**
$1/2$ cup	**uncooked long-grain white rice**
$1/4$ cup	**minced fresh parsley**
I tablespoon	**white wine vinegar**

In a medium bowl, stir together the sausage, breadcrumbs, cheese and egg. Roll into balls, about I heaping tablespoon each. Heat a large stock pot to medium-high heat. Add oil and meatballs and cook until lightly browned on all sides. Remove meatballs and set aside.

In same pot, add carrot, celery and onion and saute until softened, for 3–5 minutes. Add garlic and cook for I minute. Add meatballs, broth and rice. Bring to a simmer and cook for about 20 minutes, or until rice is tender. Stir in parsley and vinegar. Makes 6–8 servings.

CREAMLESS MUSHROOM SOUP

3 tablespoons	**butter or vegetable oil**
1/2 cup	**diced onion**
3 cloves	**garlic,** pressed
8 cups	**thinly sliced fresh mushrooms,** any variety
4 cups	**low sodium vegetable broth**
2 cups	**cooked white rice**
1 tablespoon	**white wine vinegar**
1 teaspoon	**cayenne pepper sauce**
	salt and pepper, to taste

Heat a large stock pot to medium-high heat. Add oil and onion, and saute for 2–3 minutes, until softened. Add garlic and saute for 1 minute. Add mushrooms and saute until softened, about 5–8 minutes. Remove about 1/3 of mushroom mixture, dice and then set aside. Add broth, and bring to a boil. Reduce heat and simmer covered for about 20 minutes.

Add rice to pot and blend soup with a stick blender, or in small batches in a blender. Stir in the diced mushrooms. Return to heat and simmer while adding vinegar, and pepper sauce. Season with salt and pepper. Serve warm. Makes 4–6 servings.

WILD RICE, TURKEY AND BACON SOUP

2 slices	**bacon**
2 stalks	**celery,** thinly sliced
1	**large carrot,** peeled and thinly sliced
2 tablespoons	**flour**
1 pound	**cooked turkey breast,** cut in 1-inch cubes
4 cups	**chicken broth**
2 cups	**water**
1 box (6 ounces)	**quick cooking wild rice mix**

In a large pot over medium-high heat, cook bacon until crisp and browned and all the fat is rendered. Remove bacon, dice and set aside, leaving about 2 tablespoons of bacon fat in pot. Add celery and carrot to pot and cook until softened, about 5 minutes, stirring frequently. Stir in flour until well incorporated and cook 1 minute more. Add turkey, broth and water and bring to a boil. Stir in wild rice mix with seasoning packet. Reduce heat and simmer about 5 more minutes. Makes 4–6 servings.

HAMBURGER STEW

I pound	**ground beef**
I	**medium onion,** chopped
2 cups	**diced carrots, or baby carrots**
3	**red or russet potatoes,** peeled and cubed
I can (14.5 ounces)	**diced tomatoes,** with liquid
$^1/_2$ cup	**uncooked long-grain converted rice,** not instant
I can (8 ounces)	**tomato sauce**
4 cups	**water**
2	**beef bouillon cubes**
$^1/_2$ teaspoon	**chili powder**
I teaspoon	**minced garlic**

In a large pot, brown ground beef and onion until meat is cooked through. Drain grease, if necessary. Stir in carrots, potatoes, tomatoes, rice, tomato sauce, water, bouillon cubes, chili powder and garlic. Bring soup to a boil and reduce heat to low. Simmer for I hour. Makes 6–8 servings.

STUFFED BELL PEPPER SOUP

I pound	**ground beef**
I	**green bell pepper,** seeded and chopped
I can (15 ounces)	**tomato sauce**
2 cups	**water**
I can (14.5 ounces)	**diced tomatoes with basil, garlic and oregano,** with liquid
I	**beef bouillon cube**
1/2 teaspoon	**salt**
1/2 teaspoon	**black pepper**
I 1/2 teaspoons	**soy sauce**
I 1/2 cups	**cooked white rice**

In a large pot, brown ground beef until no longer pink. Drain any excess grease if necessary. Stir in bell pepper, tomato sauce, water, tomatoes, bouillon, salt, pepper and soy sauce. Cover and simmer on low heat for 30–45 minutes. Stir in rice and heat 5 minutes more. Makes 6–8 servings.

SOUTHWESTERN CILANTRO RICE SOUP

4 cans (14 ounces each)	**beef broth**
2 cans (14.5 ounces each)	**diced tomatoes and green chiles,** with liquid
26 (1 pound)	**frozen, fully cooked meatballs**
1 cup	**chopped onion**
1/2 cup	**chopped fresh cilantro**
2 teaspoons	**Italian seasoning**
1/2 cup	**uncooked long-grain white rice**
	grated Mexican-blend cheese, optional

In a 5- to 7-quart slow cooker prepared with nonstick cooking spray, stir together broth, tomatoes, meatballs, onion, cilantro and seasoning. Sprinkle rice evenly over the top. Cover and cook over high heat for 3–4 hours or on low heat for 6–8 hours. Garnish with cheese if desired. Makes 10–12 servings.

Note: Recipe can be halved and prepared in a 3- to 4-quart slow cooker.

CHICKEN TORTILLA SOUP

I pound	**boneless, skinless chicken breast**
	salt and pepper
3 tablespoons	**vegetable oil**
$^1/_2$	**medium onion,** diced
$^1/_2$	**green bell pepper,** diced
3 cloves	**garlic,** minced
$^1/_2$ cup	**uncooked long-grain white rice**
I cup	**favorite medium or hot**
	salsa, any style
I cup	**corn**
I can (6 ounces)	**sliced black olives,** drained
I can (16 ounces)	**Ranch-style beans**
I can (8 ounces)	**tomato sauce**
4 cups	**chicken broth**
2 cups	**water**

Cut chicken into $^1/_2$-inch cubes and sprinkle with salt and pepper. Heat a large pot on medium-high heat. Add oil and chicken to pot and cook, stirring until chicken is lightly browned. Add onions and bell pepper and cook for a few more minutes, until softened. Add garlic and rice, stir and cook until garlic is fragrant and rice is coated, about I minute. Add salsa, corn, olives, beans, tomato sauce, broth and water. Reduce heat and simmer for 20 minutes. Serve with crushed tortilla chips, sour cream and green onions. Makes 4–6 servings.

POULTRY AND SEAFOOD

BALSAMIC CHICKEN STACKS

3	**partially frozen boneless, skinless chicken breasts**
1/2 cup	**balsamic vinegar**
1/4 cup	**soy sauce**
1/4 cup	**honey**
2 pounds	**fresh spinach,** coarsely chopped
16 ounces	**sliced mushrooms**
2 tablespoons	**butter or margarine**
1 teaspoon	**garlic powder**
6 cups	**hot cooked rice**

Preheat oven on broiler setting.

Lay breasts flat. With knife parallel to cutting surface, cut breasts into 2 large flat slices and place on a baking sheet. In a small bowl, mix together the vinegar, soy sauce and honey. Brush this over the chicken pieces, place in oven and broil for 6–8 minutes on each side, or until golden brown. Remove chicken from oven, brush with sauce again and then let stand for a few minutes.

Pour remaining sauce in a large frying pan or wok. Add spinach and cover pan. Cook on high heat, stirring occasionally until spinach has cooked down. In a small frying pan, saute mushrooms in butter for a few minutes to release their moisture and begin to brown; sprinkle with garlic powder.

On each serving plate, make a stack as follows: 1 cup rice, 1/2 cup spinach, 1 chicken piece, and 1/2 cup sauteed mushrooms. Makes 6 servings.

CAJUN CHICKEN AND RICE

2 tablespoons	**olive oil**
I tablespoon	**butter or margarine**
8	**skinless chicken thighs**
8 tablespoons	**Worcestershire sauce**
8 teaspoons	**Cajun spice**
I	**red bell pepper,** julienned
I	**green bell pepper,** julienned
I	**large red onion,** julienned
I cup	**water**
8 cups	**hot cooked rice**

Preheat oven to 375 degrees.

Heat the oil and butter in a large frying pan. Coat each chicken thigh with I tablespoon Worcestershire sauce and I teaspoon Cajun spice. Saute thighs for 5 minutes, turning once.

Place bell peppers and onion into a 2-quart casserole dish that has been prepared with nonstick cooking spray. Place thighs on top. Stir water into frying pan over high heat to deglaze pan. Pour liquid over top of thighs. Cover and bake for 30–40 minutes, or until vegetables are cooked through. Serve with rice. Makes 6–8 servings.

SALSA CHICKEN BOWL

2–3	**boneless, skinless chicken breasts**
1 cup	**chicken broth**
1 cup	**salsa**
1 can (15.25 ounces)	**corn,** drained
2 cans (15 ounces each)	**black beans,** rinsed and drained
1 packet (1.25 ounces)	**taco seasoning**
$^1/_2$ cup	**sour cream**
1 $^1/_4$ cups	**grated cheddar cheese**
6 cups	**hot cooked rice**

Place chicken in a 3 $^1/_2$- to 5-quart slow cooker that has been prepared with nonstick cooking spray. Pour broth, salsa, corn, beans and taco seasoning over chicken. Cover and cook on low heat 6–8 hours or on high heat 3–4 hours. Remove chicken and shred with two forks.

Stir in sour cream and cheese. Return chicken to slow cooker, mixing well. Portion cooked rice into 4–6 bowls. Spoon the chicken mixture over the rice and garnish with cheese if desired. Makes 4–6 servings.

CHICKEN GREEN CHILE BAKE

I can (14 ounces)	**chicken broth**
I cup	**uncooked medium or long-grain white rice**
I cup	**sour cream**
I can (4 ounces)	**diced green chiles**
I can (11 ounces)	**Mexicorn,** drained
I can (10 ounces or larger)	**chicken breast meat,** drained
I cup	**grated cheddar cheese,** divided

Preheat oven to 350 degrees.

In a large saucepan, bring the broth and rice to a boil. Reduce heat to low, cover, and simmer for 20 minutes, or until rice is done. Stir sour cream, chiles, Mexicorn, chicken and $1/2$ cup cheese into rice. Spoon rice mixture into an 8 x 8-inch pan that has been prepared with nonstick cooking spray. Sprinkle remaining cheese over top. Bake uncovered for 30 minutes, or until bubbly. Makes 6 servings.

TANGY CHICKEN AND RICE

2 cups	**uncooked long-grain white rice**
4 cups	**low sodium chicken broth**
I pound	**uncooked boneless, skinless chicken breasts,** cut into 2-inch cubes
I jar (8 ounces)	**apricot jam**
$^1/_4$ cup	**dried minced onion**
2 tablespoons	**beef bouillon granules**
$^1/_2$ tablespoon	**onion powder**
$^1/_2$ teaspoon	**celery seeds**
8 ounces	**Russian salad dressing**

Preheat oven to 350 degrees.

In a large saucepan, bring the rice and broth to a boil. Reduce heat and simmer for 10 minutes. Rice will be undercooked.

Generously butter a 9 x 13-inch pan. Pour rice with remaining broth into the pan. Layer the chicken over top of rice.

In a small bowl, mix together the jam, onion, bouillon, onion powder and celery seeds. Pour over chicken and then pour the dressing evenly over top. Cover and bake for 60 minutes. Uncover and bake another 20–30 minutes, until bubbling on top and rice is cooked through. Makes 4–6 servings.

BACON RANCH
CHICKEN AND RICE

1 pound	**boneless, skinless chicken breasts**
1 cup	**chopped onion**
4 tablespoons	**real bacon bits**
2 teaspoons	**minced garlic**
1 envelope	**Ranch dressing mix**
2 cans (10.75 ounces each)	**cream of chicken soup,** condensed
1 cup	**sour cream**
1/2 cup	**milk**
8 cups	**hot cooked rice**

Prepare a 3 1/2- to 5-quart slow cooker with nonstick cooking spray, and layer chicken, onion, and bacon bits into the bottom.

In a medium bowl, combine garlic, dressing mix and soups. Spoon soup mixture over the chicken. Cover and cook 6–8 hours on low, or 3–4 hours on high. During last hour, shred chicken before stirring in sour cream and milk. Serve over hot rice. Makes 6–8 servings.

HAWAIIAN HAYSTACKS

10–12	**chicken breast tenders,** cut into chunks
1 cup	**chicken broth**
2 cans (10.75 ounces each)	**cream of chicken soup,** condensed
1 can (12 ounces)	**evaporated milk**
6 cups	**hot cooked rice**
	toppings of choice

Place chicken in a 3 1/2- to 5-quart slow cooker that has been prepared with nonstick cooking spray. In a large bowl, whisk together the broth, soups and evaporated milk until smooth. Pour evenly over the chicken. Cover and cook on high heat for 3–4 hours, or on low heat 6–8 hours.

Serve over rice with a variety of toppings such as, grated cheddar cheese, peas, pineapple tidbits, shredded coconut, chow mein noodles, sliced olives, diced tomatoes, diced bell pepper or sliced green onions. Makes 4–6 servings.

ORANGE RICE
AND ORANGE CHICKEN

3	**boneless, skinless chicken breasts,** cut into $^1/_2$-inch pieces
4 cups	**Panda Express Orange Sauce,** divided
1 $^1/_2$ cups	**flour**
$^1/_4$ teaspoon	**salt**
$^1/_4$ teaspoon	**pepper**
$^1/_3$ cup	**vegetable or olive oil**

Orange Rice:

$^1/_2$ cup	**diced onion**
1 tablespoon	**olive oil**
juice and zest of 1	**orange**
$^1/_2$ teaspoon	**ground ginger**
4 cups	**hot cooked rice**

Place chicken pieces in a gallon-size ziplock bag. Pour 1 $^1/_4$ cup sauce over chicken, seal bag and marinate chicken in refrigerator for at least 2 hours. In a separate gallon-size ziplock bag, combine flour, salt and pepper. Add the marinated chicken pieces to flour, seal and shake to coat the chicken. Heat oil in a large frying pan over medium-high heat, add floured chicken and cook until browned. Remove and place chicken on a plate covered with paper towels to absorb excess grease. Cover with aluminum foil to keep warm. Clean the frying pan.

In a large saucepan, heat remaining orange sauce. In the large frying pan, saute onion in olive oil until soft. Turn heat to low and stir in juice, zest and ginger. Cook for 30 seconds. Stir in cooked rice and simmer for 1−2 minutes, until excess liquid has been absorbed into rice. Stir chicken into hot orange sauce and serve over rice. Makes 4 servings.

CHICKEN TERIYAKI CASSEROLE

1 pound	**boneless, skinless chicken tenders**
1/2 cup	**teriyaki marinade**
2 tablespoons	**vegetable oil**
1 cup	**thinly sliced celery**
1 cup	**thinly sliced carrots**
1 cup	**small broccoli florets**
2 cups	**cooked rice**
1 can (8 ounces)	**sliced water chestnuts**
1 cup	**chicken broth**
3	**green onions,** thinly sliced

Preheat oven to 350 degrees.

Place chicken between 2 sheets of plastic wrap and pound to a uniform 1/2-inch thickness. Place in a large ziplock bag with marinade and refrigerate for 30 minutes.

Remove chicken from bag, shaking to remove excess marinade, reserving the marinade. Heat oil in a large frying pan and cook chicken until browned on both sides, 3–5 minutes per side. Remove chicken from pan and set aside. To same frying pan, add the celery, carrots and broccoli; saute for 3–5 minutes until slightly softened.

In a large bowl, stir together the carrot mixture, rice, water chestnuts, broth and remaining teriyaki marinade. Spread into a 9 x 13-inch pan that has been prepared with nonstick cooking spray. Scatter green onions over top. Slice cooked chicken into 1-inch slices and spread evenly over top. Cover and bake 20 minutes. Uncover and bake for another 5 minutes. Makes 4–6 servings.

CHICKEN CURRY

1 can (14 ounces)	**coconut milk**
2 tablespoons	**green or red curry paste,** or to taste
2–3	**boneless, skinless chicken breasts**
2 tablespoons	**brown sugar**
2 cans (8 ounces each)	**sliced bamboo shoots**
1 cup	**frozen peas**
6 cups	**hot cooked rice**

In a large frying pan, bring coconut milk and curry paste to a simmer. Cut chicken into bite-size pieces and add to pan. Simmer for 10 minutes, stirring frequently. Add remaining ingredients except rice and simmer another 10–15 minutes, stirring frequently, or until sauce thickens. Serve curry over cooked rice. Makes 6 servings.

CHICKEN STIR-FRY

2 pounds	**boneless, skinless chicken breasts**
3 tablespoons	**soy sauce**
1 teaspoon	**garlic powder**
1/4 cup	**cornstarch**
1/4 cup	**olive or canola oil**
8 cups	**chopped fresh vegetables,** such as broccoli, carrots and celery
1 jar (12 ounces)	**stir-fry sauce**
1/2 cup	**water**
6 cups	**hot cooked rice**

Chop chicken into small pieces and place in a gallon-size ziplock bag. In a small bowl, mix together soy sauce, garlic powder and cornstarch and pour over chicken. Set aside at room temperature, turning frequently, up to 30 minutes.

Heat oil in a wok or large frying pan. Add vegetables and stir-fry for a few minutes, or until slightly softened but still a little firm; add chicken. Cook for a few more minutes. Add stir-fry sauce and water. Cook until heated through and chicken is no longer pink. If sauce is not thickened to your liking, mix a little cornstarch and water together and stir into mixture, cooking until thickened. Serve over rice. Makes 6-8 servings.

Garlic Chicken Variation: After oil is heated, stir in 2–3 tablespoons minced fresh garlic and cook until lightly browned. Add remaining ingredients, omitting stir-fry sauce and adding 1/2 cup water.

Ginger Chicken Variation: After oil is heated, add 2–3 tablespoons grated fresh ginger and cook until limp. Add remaining ingredients, omitting stir-fry sauce and adding 1/2 cup water.

CHICKEN SOFT TACOS

1 pound	**boneless, skinless chicken breasts,** sliced into thin strips
1 tablespoon	**olive oil**
2 cups	**water**
1 cup	**chunky salsa**
1 packet (1.25 ounces)	**taco seasoning**
1 can (15 ounces)	**black beans,** drained and rinsed
2 cups	**uncooked instant white rice**
8–10	**6-inch flour tortillas**
⅔ cup	**grated cheddar cheese**

In a large frying pan, saute chicken strips for 4–5 minutes in hot olive oil, stirring occasionally until cooked through. Add water and salsa. Stir in taco seasoning and black beans. Bring mixture to a boil and stir in rice. Reduce heat to low, cover, and cook for 5 minutes.

Spoon chicken rice mixture evenly onto tortillas. Sprinkle cheese over filling before folding sides. Serve with shredded lettuce, diced tomatoes or salsa, sour cream or other favorite toppings. Makes 4–5 servings.

ASIAN LETTUCE WRAPS

1	**red bell pepper,** diced
1 tablespoon	**vegetable oil**
1 pound	**ground chicken or turkey**
2 teaspoons	**grated fresh ginger**
2 cups	**cooked white rice**
1 cup	**chicken broth**
1 tablespoon	**chili garlic sauce**
1 tablespoon	**soy sauce**
1 tablespoon	**brown sugar**
1 teaspoon	**cornstarch**
3	**green onions,** thinly sliced
2 tablespoons	**minced cilantro**
1 head	**Bibb lettuce**

Heat a large frying pan to medium-high heat and saute bell pepper in oil for about 3 minutes. Add ground chicken and cook until chicken is browned. Stir in ginger and cook for 1 minute. Stir in rice until well incorporated.

In a small bowl, whisk together the broth, chili sauce, soy sauce, brown sugar and cornstarch. Add to frying pan and cook until mixture has thickened, about 1 minute. Stir in green onions and cilantro. Serve with leaves of Bibb lettuce for wraps. Makes 4 servings.

MUSHROOM AND ARTICHOKE CHICKEN

8 ounces	**sliced fresh mushrooms**
2 tablespoons	**butter or vegetable oil**
I cup	**chopped onion**
I cup	**chopped red bell pepper**
1/4 cup	**cornstarch**
2–2 1/2	**cups chicken broth,** divided
I teaspoon	**Italian seasoning**
I box (6 ounces)	**long-grain and wild rice mix,** cooked according to package directions
2 cups	**cubed, cooked chicken**
I can (14 ounces)	**artichoke hearts,** drained and quartered
I cup	**grated mozzarella cheese**

Preheat oven to 350 degrees.

In a large frying pan, saute mushrooms in melted butter until tender. Add onion and bell pepper and saute, stirring occasionally until tender.

In a small bowl, whisk together cornstarch, 2 cups broth and Italian seasoning. Add broth mixture to frying pan. Stirring constantly, cook over medium heat for about 3 minutes until sauce thickens. Fold in cooked rice and chicken and simmer until thoroughly heated. If mixture is too thick, add more broth as needed.

Spoon mixture evenly into a 9 x 13-inch baking pan that has been prepared with nonstick cooking spray. Evenly spread quartered artichoke hearts over top and sprinkle with cheese. Bake covered with aluminum foil for 25 minutes. Uncover and bake an additional 10–15 minutes, until bubbly. Makes 6–8 servings.

TURKEY SALAD CROISSANTS

³/₄ cup	**light mayonnaise**
I tablespoon	**apple cider vinegar**
2 teaspoons	**sugar or sugar substitute**
I ¹/₂ cups	**leftover cooked rice,** any variety
2 cups	**cubed, cooked turkey**
¹/₃ cup	**diced green onion**
I ¹/₄ cups	**seedless red grapes,** halved
	slivered almonds, optional
6	**croissants**

In a large bowl, mix together mayonnaise, vinegar and sugar. Fold in rice, turkey, onions and grapes until everything is evenly coated. Season with salt and pepper, to taste. Cover and refrigerate for a minimum of 2 hours, or until ready to serve. Stir almonds into salad before serving, if desired. Slice croissants and fill with salad right before serving. Makes 6 servings.

SHRIMP FRIED RICE

1 pound (26–30 count)	**uncooked shrimp,** peeled and deveined
2 teaspoons	**cornstarch**
1/4 teaspoon	**salt**
1/4 teaspoon	**pepper**
3 1/2 tablespoons	**olive oil,** divided
4	**eggs,** beaten
1/3 cup	**chopped green onion**
5 cups	**cold cooked rice**
1 package (12 ounces)	**frozen carrots and peas,** thawed and drained
4 tablespoons	**soy sauce,** divided

Place shrimp, cornstarch, salt and pepper in a gallon-size ziplock bag. Seal bag and toss until shrimp is coated. Allow shrimp to sit in bag for 10 minutes at room temperature.

In a large wok or frying pan, saute shrimp in 2 tablespoons hot olive oil on high for 2–3 minutes on each side, or until shrimp is thoroughly cooked. Place cooked shrimp in a bowl. Reduce heat to medium and pour beaten eggs into the same pan, scrambling into small pieces until no longer runny. Spoon cooked eggs into a separate bowl.

Wash out pan. Heat 1 1/2 tablespoons oil in clean pan over high heat. Stir in green onion and saute for 1 minute. Add rice to onions, stirring occasionally until rice is thoroughly heated. Drizzle 3 tablespoons soy sauce over rice and mix well. Fold in vegetables and cook for 2 more minutes. Fold in cooked shrimp and eggs and heat until rice mixture is hot, stirring every 20–30 seconds. Drizzle remaining tablespoon of soy sauce over top. Serve immediately. Makes 6–8 servings.

MANGO MAHI MAHI AND COCONUT RICE

4	**mahi mahi fillets**
I bottle (12 ounces)	**Hawaiian or Sesame Ginger Marinade**
2 cups	**uncooked jasmine rice**
2 cups	**chicken broth**
I tablespoon	**butter or margarine**
¾ can (14 ounces)	**coconut milk**
2 tablespoons	**sugar**

Mango Salsa:

I ½ teaspoons	**butter or margarine**
I ½ tablespoons	**sugar**
I ½ cups	**cubed fresh mango**

Place mahi mahi in a large bowl with a lid. Pour marinade over fillets, cover and toss to coat. Refrigerate for 1–4 hours.

Preheat oven on broiler setting.

In a large saucepan, bring rice, broth, butter and coconut milk to a boil. Reduce heat to medium-low, stir and cover. Simmer for about 20 minutes, or until liquid is absorbed. Stir in sugar. While rice is cooking, shake excess marinade off mahi mahi and place fillets in a large baking dish. Broil uncovered for 10–15 minutes until the fish flakes easily with a fork.

To make salsa, heat butter and sugar in a small saucepan over medium heat. When sugar starts to bubble, stir in mango. Cook stirring frequently for 5 minutes, or until mango is tender. Serve mahi mahi over rice and garnish with mango salsa. Makes 4 servings.

BEEF AND PORK

BEEF AND MUSHROOMS

2 pounds	**stew meat,** cubed
2 cans (10.75 ounces each)	**cream of mushroom soup,** condensed
2 cans (4 ounces each)	**mushroom pieces,** drained
1 cup	**apple juice**
1 package (1 ounce)	**dry onion soup mix**
6 cups	**hot cooked rice**

Combine all ingredients except rice in a 3 1/2- to 5-quart slow cooker
that has been prepared with nonstick cooking spray. Cover and cook
on low heat for 8–10 hours. Ladle beef and mushrooms over hot rice.
Makes 4–6 servings.

PINEAPPLE MEATBALLS AND RICE

¹/₂ cup	**brown sugar**
1 ¹/₂ tablespoons	**cornstarch**
I can (20 ounces)	**pineapple chunks,** drained, juice reserved
¹/₃ cup	**rice vinegar**
I tablespoon	**soy sauce**
I	**green bell pepper,** seeded and chopped
13	**frozen pre-cooked meatballs,** thawed
4 cups	**hot cooked rice**

In a large saucepan, combine brown sugar and cornstarch. Stir in reserved pineapple juice, vinegar and soy sauce and bring to a boil, stirring every 2 minutes.

Add bell pepper and meatballs to the sauce and return to a boil. Reduce heat to medium-high, cover and simmer for 5 minutes. Stir and reduce heat to medium. Stir in pineapple chunks and simmer 5 minutes more. Serve over hot rice. Makes 2–3 servings.

SWEET AND SOUR BEEF

2 pounds	**stew meat,** cubed
1 bottle (10 ounces)	**sweet-and-sour sauce**
1	**green bell pepper,** cut into $3/4$-inch pieces
$1/2$	**onion,** cut into $1/2$-inch pieces
4–6 cups	**hot cooked rice**

Combine all ingredients except rice in a 2- to $3\,1/2$-quart slow cooker that has been prepared with nonstick cooking spray. Cover and cook on low heat 6–8 hours. Serve over hot rice. Makes 4–6 servings.

HAWAIIAN FRIED RICE

3 tablespoons	**soy sauce**
1 tablespoon	**sesame oil**
1 teaspoon	**cayenne pepper sauce**
1 tablespoon	**vegetable oil**
2 cups	**diced ham or Spam**
1	**red bell pepper,** diced
6	**green onions,** thinly sliced, whites and greens divided
3 cloves	**garlic,** minced
5 cups	**cooked white rice,** chilled
3	**eggs,** beaten
1 can (8 ounces)	**pineapple tidbits,** drained

In a small bowl combine the soy sauce, sesame oil and pepper sauce.

In a large frying pan, heat the vegetable oil over medium-high heat. Add diced ham, bell pepper and whites of green onions. Saute for about 5 minutes, until peppers are fork tender. Add garlic and saute 1 more minute.

Break up rice with fingers while adding to frying pan. Cook for about 5 more minutes, stirring frequently until rice is heated through. Push rice to edges of pan, add eggs to center and scramble until cooked through. Stir everything together in frying pan, remove from heat and stir in pineapple and remaining green onions. Makes 6–8 servings.

HAMBURGER SALSA SKILLET

1 pound	**ground beef**
1 can (14.5 ounces)	**fire-roasted diced tomatoes,** with liquid
1 can (15.25 ounces)	**black beans,** rinsed and drained
1 cup	**uncooked long-grain white rice**
1 can (14.5 ounces)	**beef broth**
$^2/_3$ cup	**salsa**
1 teaspoon	**chili powder**

In a large frying pan, brown ground beef until no longer pink. Drain any excess grease if necessary. Stir remaining ingredients into cooked beef. Bring to a boil. Reduce heat to low. Cover and simmer for 20–25 minutes, or until rice is done. Let stand 5 minutes before serving. Makes 4–6 servings.

DINNER MADE EASY

I pound	**ground beef or sausage**
I	**medium onion,** chopped
I can (4 ounces)	**sliced mushrooms,** drained
I	**green, red or yellow bell pepper**, seeded and chopped
3 cups	**hot cooked rice**
	soy sauce

In a large frying pan, brown ground meat until no longer pink. Drain any excess grease if necessary. Stir onion, mushrooms and bell pepper into beef. Saute until onions are transparent. Stir in cooked rice. Top individual servings with desired amount of soy sauce. Makes 4–6 servings.

BROCCOLI BEEF STIR-FRY

I pound	**top round or sirloin steak**
I tablespoon	**minced garlic**
I tablespoon	**minced fresh ginger***
4 tablespoons	**cornstarch,** divided
2 tablespoons	**soy sauce**
2 tablespoons	**peanut oil**
4 cups	**diced fresh broccoli**
1/2	**red bell pepper,** sliced into thin strips
I can (10.75 ounces)	**French onion soup,** condensed
8 cups	**hot cooked rice**

Slice beef into very thin strips and place in a small bowl. Stir garlic, ginger, 2 tablespoons cornstarch and soy sauce into beef. Let sit on counter at room temperature for 20 minutes to marinate.

Heat oil in a large frying pan or wok. Saute beef for about 2 minutes, stirring occasionally. Add broccoli and bell pepper and cook for another 2 minutes, stirring occasionally. Drain a little of the broth from the soup into a small bowl and mix remaining cornstarch into broth. Add cornstarch mixture and remainder of soup to pan. Stir and cook another 3–5 minutes, or until sauce has thickened slightly. Serve over hot rice. Makes 6–8 servings.

* I teaspoon dried ground ginger can be substituted for minced fresh ginger.

UNSTUFFED BEEF AND CABBAGE

1	**small cabbage,** shredded
2 pounds	**lean ground beef**
1	**large yellow onion,** diced
1 tablespoon	**minced garlic**
2 teaspoons	**seasoned salt**
1 can (26 ounces)	**tomato soup,** condensed
1 tablespoon	**Worcestershire sauce**
2 tablespoons	**brown sugar**
2 cups	**hot cooked rice**

Preheat oven to 375 degrees.

In a large stockpot, bring about 2 quarts water to a boil. Turn off heat and add cabbage. Let stand 10 minutes to soften and then drain.

In a large frying pan or wok, cook the ground beef over medium-high heat until it is no longer pink, about 5 minutes, stirring frequently to break up clumps. Add onion, garlic and salt. Cook another 2–3 minutes, or until onion is limp. Stir in soup, Worcestershire sauce and brown sugar.

In a 4-quart casserole dish, layer $1/3$ of the cabbage, 1 cup rice, and $1/2$ of the meat mixture; repeat layers and top with remaining cabbage. Cover and bake 45 minutes. Uncover and bake another 15 minutes. Makes 8–10 servings.

AUNT LEARA'S ZUCCHINI BOATS

4	**medium zucchini**
I pound	**ground beef or sausage**
1/2	**medium onion,** chopped
I can (8 ounces)	**tomato sauce**
2/3 cup	**cooked rice**
I 1/2 teaspoons	**Italian seasoning**
	salt
I 1/2 cups	**grated mozzarella cheese**

Preheat oven to 350 degrees.

Peel zucchini. Cut in half length-wise and then scoop out seeds to form a boat.

Bring a large pot of salted water to a boil. Boil zucchini for 5 minutes. Remove zucchini and drain. Place in bottom of a 9 x 13-inch pan.

In a large frying pan, brown ground meat and onion until meat is no longer pink. Drain excess grease if necessary. Stir in tomato sauce, rice, and Italian seasoning. Salt to taste. Fill zucchini with meat mixture. Sprinkle cheese evenly over top. Bake 20 minutes, or until heated through and cheese has melted. Makes 4–6 servings.

BACON AND EGG FRIED RICE

6 slices	**bacon,** cut into bite-size pieces
6	**green onions,** thinly sliced
I teaspoon	**minced garlic**
2	**eggs,** beaten
4 cups	**cold cooked rice**
2 1/2 tablespoons	**soy sauce**

In a large wok or frying pan, fry bacon pieces until crisp. Add onion and garlic, and stir-fry for I minute. Add beaten eggs and scramble until eggs crumble and are thoroughly cooked. Add rice and stir-fry stirring constantly until rice is heated through. Sprinkle soy sauce evenly over top and stir until soy sauce is mixed into rice mixture. Serve as a side dish or as burrito filling wrapped in a tortilla topped with your favorite salsa. Makes 4 servings.

SLOW COOKER CAJUN RED BEANS AND RICE

1 pound	**dried kidney beans***
1	**yellow onion,** diced
3 cloves	**garlic,** minced
1 pound	**andouille sausage,** diced
2 tablespoons	**cayenne pepper sauce**
3 cups	**chicken broth**
6 cups	**hot cooked white rice**
	salt and pepper, to taste

Soak beans overnight in water. Drain and place in a 4-quart slow cooker.

Stir in the onion, garlic, sausage, pepper sauce and broth. Cook on low for 6–7 hours, or on high for 3–4 hours. Season with salt and pepper. To serve, spoon rice into shallow bowls and top with bean mixture. Makes 4–6 servings.

*Note: You can substitute 2 cans (15 ounces each) drained kidney beans, but you will need to stir them into the slow cooker 1 hour before serving, instead of at the beginning of the cook time.

PORK CHOP AND RICE BAKE

1 cup	**uncooked long-grain converted rice**
4	**boneless pork chops**
2 tablespoons	**olive oil**
3 cups	**water**
1 can (10.75 ounces)	**cream of mushroom soup,** condensed
1 package (1 ounce)	**dry onion soup mix**

Preheat oven to 375 degrees.

Sprinkle rice over the bottom of an 8 x 8-inch baking pan that has been prepared with nonstick cooking spray.

In a large frying pan, brown pork chops in hot olive oil for 2 minutes on each side. Place pork chops in pan over rice, reserving any drippings. Stir water, soup and soup mix into the drippings in the frying pan. Stir and cook until hot. Pour sauce over pork chops and rice. Cover pan with aluminum foil and bake for 45 minutes. Remove foil and bake until the pork is no longer pink in the center, another 10–15 minutes. Makes 4 servings.

AROUND
THE WORLD
ENTREES

WEEKNIGHT
SKILLET PAELLA (SPAIN)

2 tablespoons	**oil**
2 teaspoons	**turmeric**
2	**large shallots,** minced
3 cloves	**garlic,** minced
4 ounces	**uncooked sweet Italian sausage,** casings removed
1 1/2 cups	**uncooked short or medium-grain white rice**
1 1/2 cups	**chicken broth**
1/2 cup	**chopped sun-dried tomatoes**
4	**boneless, skinless chicken thighs,** chopped
4 ounces	**uncooked large shrimp,** peeled and deveined
1/2 cup	**frozen peas**

Preheat oven to 425 degrees.

Heat a 10-inch oven-safe frying pan to medium-high heat. Add oil, turmeric and shallots. Cook for 2 minutes, and then add garlic and sausage. Stir constantly, breaking sausage into small bits, until sausage is browned. Stir in rice, broth and tomatoes. Place chicken pieces on top, nestling them into the rice mixture.

Bake for 50 minutes. Remove from oven and top with the shrimp and peas. Bake for another 10 minutes. Makes 6–8 servings.

ARROZ CON POLLO (PUERTO RICO)

2 tablespoons	**minced garlic**
2 tablespoons	**red wine vinegar**
I teaspoon	**salt**
8	**boneless, skinless chicken thighs**
2 tablespoons	**vegetable oil**
I	**medium onion,** diced
I	**green bell pepper,** diced
$^1/_2$ teaspoon	**red pepper flakes**
2 cups	**reduced sodium chicken broth**
I can (8 ounces)	**tomato sauce**
3 cups	**uncooked long-grain white rice**
$^1/_2$ cup	**diced green olives**
I tablespoon	**capers**
I jar (4 ounces)	**diced pimientos**

Preheat oven to 350 degrees.

In a small bowl, mix together the garlic, vinegar, and salt, and place in a large ziplock bag. Add chicken and let sit on countertop for 30 minutes, turning occasionally.

Heat a large oven-safe frying pan or Dutch oven to medium-high heat. Add oil, onion, bell pepper and pepper flakes. Cook for 5–8 minutes, stirring constantly until vegetables are softened. Push the vegetables to the edges of the pan and add chicken. Cook for 3 minutes on each side.

Stir in broth and tomato sauce and simmer for 20 minutes. Stir in rice; cover and bake for 30 minutes, or until chicken is done. Remove chicken pieces from pan and place on a serving plate. Stir the olives, capers and pimientos into the rice before serving. Makes 4–6 servings.

BIBIMBAP BOWL (KOREA)

2 cups	**bean sprouts**
1	**large carrot,** peeled and cut in thin matchsticks
1/2	**English cucumber,** cut in thin matchsticks
1 cup	**rice vinegar**
1/4 cup	**sugar**
4 cups	**hot cooked white rice**
3 tablespoons	**vegetable oil,** divided
1 teaspoon	**sesame oil**
8 ounces	**sirloin steak,** cut in 1/4 inch slices
1 tablespoon	**soy sauce**
8 ounces	**shiitake or cremini mushroom caps,** thinly sliced
3 cloves	**garlic,** pressed
10 ounces	**chopped fresh baby spinach**
	salt and pepper, to taste
4	**eggs**

Toss together the bean sprouts, carrot, cucumber, vinegar and sugar in a large ziplock bag and refrigerate 1–4 hours. Divide the rice into 4 large serving bowls and spread evenly in bottom of bowls. Drain the vegetables and place on top of rice. Heat a frying pan to medium-high heat and add 2 tablespoons of vegetable oil and sesame oil. Add beef, soy sauce and mushrooms and cook until beef is done and mushrooms are softened. Divide the mixture and place in each of the 4 bowls. In the same frying pan, add the garlic and spinach and saute until spinach is just wilted, about 1 minute; season with salt and pepper. Divide the spinach and place in each of the 4 bowls. Wipe frying pan clean. Add 1 tablespoon of vegetable oil to frying pan and reduce to medium-low heat. Crack eggs into frying pan and cover and cook for a few minutes, until whites of eggs are cooked but yolk is still runny. Place an egg over the spinach in each serving bowl. Makes 4 servings.

FORBIDDEN RICE (CHINA)

3 tablespoons	**coconut oil**
1	**small yellow onion,** diced
1	**carrot,** peeled and diced
3	**green onions,** thinly sliced
3 cloves	**garlic,** minced
1 tablespoon	**minced fresh ginger**
3 tablespoons	**soy sauce**
2 teaspoons	**sesame oil**
1 teaspoon	**Sriracha sauce**
3 cups	**cooked black rice,** cooled

In a large frying pan or wok, heat the coconut oil over medium-high heat. Add the onion and carrot, and saute for about 5 minutes, or until fork tender. Add the green onions, garlic and ginger and saute another 2 minutes. Add the soy sauce, sesame oil and Sriracha sauce. Stir in rice until well combined. Makes 6–8 servings.

PINEAPPLE FRIED RICE (THAILAND)

I tablespoon	**fish sauce,** or low sodium soy sauce
2 teaspoons	**curry powder**
I teaspoon	**cayenne pepper sauce**
I can (8 ounces)	**pineapple tidbits,** juice reserved
2 tablespoons	**vegetable oil**
2 ounces	**finely diced ham**
2	**green onions,** thinly sliced
3 cloves	**garlic,** minced
I	**egg,** beaten
I cup	**frozen peas and carrots,** thawed
1/2 cup	**roasted salted cashew pieces**
3 cups	**cold cooked white rice**
1/3 cup	**diced fresh cilantro**

In a small bowl, stir together the fish sauce, curry powder, pepper sauce and reserved pineapple juice. Set aside.

Heat a large frying pan to medium-high heat. Add oil. Add ham and green onions and saute for 2 minutes. Add garlic and saute for I more minute. Make a well in the center of the frying pan and add the egg. Cook and scramble until no longer runny. Add the peas, carrots and cashews.

Break up rice with fingers and add to frying pan. Drizzle in the fish sauce mixture and stir until rice has evenly absorbed liquid. Remove from heat and stir in pineapple tidbits. Serve garnished with cilantro. Makes 4–6 servings.

ARANCINI RICE BALLS (SICILY)

4 cups	**cooked Calrose white rice,** cooled
1 cup	**grated Parmesan cheese**
5	**eggs,** divided
16	**small cubes fresh mozzarella cheese**
1 1/4 cups	**seasoned breadcrumbs**
	oil for frying
2 cups	**marinara sauce**

Combine the rice, Parmesan cheese, and 3 eggs in a large bowl. Mix well with hands. Form 16 arancini by taking a small amount of the rice mixture, and stuffing 1 cube of mozzarella inside each ball, squeezing the rice mixture firmly around the cheese. Squeezing the arancini together tightly will ensure that the balls hold their shape when frying.

In a separate bowl, whisk together remaining 2 eggs. In a different bowl, add breadcrumbs. Dip each rice ball in the egg mixture and then in the breadcrumbs.

In a large pot, heat 4 inches of oil until oil reaches 375 degrees. Drop 3 or 4 balls into hot oil. Fry until golden brown and cooked thoroughly. Remove with a slotted spoon and place fried arancini on a plate lined with paper towels. Season with salt if desired. Repeat the process until all 16 arancini are cooked. Serve with heated marinara sauce on the side. Makes 4–5 servings.

FRAGRANT STUFFED GRAPE LEAVES (GREECE)

1/4 cup	**oil**
1	**onion,** chopped
1/2 cup	**diced dried apricots**
1 cup	**cooked rice**
1/2 cup	**cooked lentils**
1/2 cup	**chopped fresh parsley**
1/4 cup	**chopped fresh mint**
1/2 teaspoon	**cinnamon**
1/4 teaspoon	**nutmeg**
1 teaspoon	**salt**
juice and zest of 1	**lemon**
18	**grape leaves,** from a jar, rinsed*

Add the oil to a large Dutch oven or frying pan and cook the onion and apricots over medium-high heat until the onion is translucent. Add remaining ingredients except grape leaves and stir and cook for another few minutes, until well combined and heated through. Remove stuffing from the pan to a separate dish.

Place a grape leaf (or kale leaf) vein-side up, with the stem facing you. Remove stem with a knife. Put 2 heaping tablespoons of filling at the base of the leaf, and arrange into a horizontal line. Fold the base end of the leaf over the filling, tuck in the sides and roll into a cigar shape. Repeat with remaining leaves and stuffing. Place the stuffed grape leaves in the Dutch oven or frying pan so that they are touching. Pour enough water into pan to completely cover grape leaves by 1 inch. Place a glass plate firmly on top of the bundles, to keep them submerged while cooking. Bring to a boil, reduce heat and simmer for about 30 minutes, or until tender. Makes 4–6 servings.

*A great substitute for grape leaves is fresh kale leaves.

MUJADDARA LENTILS AND RICE (MIDDLE EAST)

I cup	**uncooked long-grain brown rice**
2 cups	**green lentils,** rinsed
I cup	**Greek yogurt**
2 teaspoons	**cumin,** divided
I tablespoon	**lemon juice**
2 teaspoons	**lemon zest**
I teaspoon	**coriander**
3 tablespoons	**olive oil,** divided
3	**large onions,** peeled
1/2 teaspoon	**cinnamon**
I teaspoon	**salt**
	freshly ground black pepper, to taste
I cup	**finely chopped fresh flat-leaf parsley**

Place the rice in a large saucepan with 2 cups of water and a dash of salt. Bring to a boil, reduce to a simmer, cover and cook for 45–50 minutes. In another large saucepan, cover the lentils with 2 inches of water, and bring to a boil. Continue boiling for 20–25 minutes, until tender; remove from heat and drain.

In a small bowl, whisk together the yogurt, I teaspoon cumin, lemon juice, lemon zest, and coriander.

In a large frying pan, heat I tablespoon olive oil on medium-high heat. Slice the onions into thin slices from top to bottom, making long thin strips. Add onion strips to frying pan. Reduce heat to low and cook for about 25 minutes, stirring occasionally. Place cooked rice, lentils and onions in a large serving dish and toss together with I teaspoon cumin, cinnamon, salt, remaining olive oil and parsley. Drizzle yogurt mixture over the lentils and rice mixture when serving. Makes 4–6 servings.

SUSHI RICE BOWLS (JAPAN)

$^1/_2$	**English cucumber**
4 ounces	**cooked chilled crab meat**
$^1/_2$	**large avocado**
1 tablespoon	**lemon juice**
$^1/_4$ cup	**seasoned rice vinegar**
1 teaspoon	**sesame oil**
1 tablespoon	**sugar**
1–2 teaspoons	**wasabi paste,** optional
3 cups	**warm cooked white rice**
2 sheets	**nori (dried seaweed),** optional
2 tablespoons	**sesame seeds**

Cut cucumber in half lengthwise and scoop out seeds with a spoon. Dice the cucumber into very small pieces, about the size of peas. Dice crab meat. Dice avocado and toss with lemon juice.

In a small bowl, mix together the vinegar, oil and sugar, and the wasabi paste (if using). In a large bowl, toss rice with vinegar mixture, using hands if needed to distribute vinegar evenly. Let rice cool to room temperature. Cut nori sheets (if using) into very thin julienne strips.

Add nori, cucumber, crab and avocado to rice; toss to combine. Divide into serving bowls and sprinkle with sesame seeds. Makes 4 servings.

RICE STUFFED OMELET ROLLS (JAPAN)

2 tablespoons	**cream cheese,** at room temperature
I tablespoon	**flour**
$1/4$ teaspoon	**salt**
$1/3$ cup	**whole milk,** at room temperature
6	**eggs,** at room temperature
$1/2$	**red bell pepper,** julienned
4	**thin asparagus spears**
$1/2$ cup	**finely grated Parmesan cheese**
$1/2$ cup	**cooked rice**
	sesame seeds for garnish

Preheat oven to 350 degrees.

Line the bottom and sides of a 9 x 13-inch baking pan with aluminum foil so that the edges are hanging over the pan, forming a sling. Spray with nonstick cooking spray and set aside.

In a small bowl add cream cheese, flour and salt. Whisk until combined. Slowly whisk in milk until smooth. Beat in the eggs until blended and pour into prepared pan. Bake for 30–35 minutes, or until eggs are puffed and set. While the egg mixture is cooking, blanch or microwave the bell pepper slices and asparagus until slightly softened, but still firm.

Remove egg mixture from the oven and use foil to lift egg from the pan. Sprinkle with cheese, and sprinkle rice evenly over top, I inch from the edge of the long side closest to you, forming a rice rectangle. Place bell pepper strips and asparagus spears on rice, forming a line across the egg. Roll up from large side, using foil as a help. Let sit for a few minutes to cool and firm. Slice into 2-inch pieces, and place cut sides up on a serving plate. Sprinkle with the sesame seeds and serve. Makes 4–6 servings.

BURRITO RICE BOWLS (MEXICO)

1 tablespoon	**vegetable oil**
1 pound	**85% lean ground beef**
1 tablespoon	**chili powder**
1 tablespoon	**cumin**
$^1/_2$	**onion,** diced
3 cloves	**garlic,** minced
1	**jalapeno pepper,** seeded and diced
1 can (15 ounces)	**diced tomatoes,** with liquid
2 tablespoons	**hot sauce**
4 cups	**hot cooked rice**
4 ounces	**grated cheddar cheese**
	salsa, for garnish

Heat the vegetable oil in a large frying pan to medium-high heat. Add the ground beef and stir until cooked through, breaking into small bits as it cooks. Add the chili powder, cumin and onions and cook for a few minutes, until onions are softened. Add garlic and jalapeno and cook a few more minutes, until jalapeno is fork tender. Stir in tomatoes and hot sauce. Simmer until mixture has thickened and very little liquid remains. Spoon rice into serving bowls and top with beef mixture. Garnish with cheese and salsa. Makes 4–6 servings.

BOLINHOS DE ARROZ FRITTERS (BRAZIL)

1/2 cup	**flour**
1 teaspoon	**baking powder**
1/4 teaspoon	**salt**
1	**egg,** beaten
1/4 cup	**milk**
1/3 cup	**finely chopped onion**
2 tablespoons	**chopped fresh parsley***
1/2 cup	**grated Parmesan cheese**
2 cups	**leftover rice**
	canola or vegetable oil, for frying

In a small bowl, combine flour, baking powder and salt.

In a large bowl, stir together beaten egg, milk, onion, parsley, cheese and rice. Stir in flour mixture.

Heat 2–3 inches of oil in a heavy pot to approximately 360–375 degrees. Fry rounded tablespoons of batter in hot oil for 2–3 minutes until golden brown. Place fried fritters on a plate lined with paper towels. Season with salt to taste. Makes 15 fritters.

* 2 teaspoons dried parsley can be used in place of fresh parsley.

CANJA SOUP (BRAZIL)

2–3	**boneless, skinless chicken breasts**
8 cups	**chicken broth**
I	**large onion,** chopped
3	**carrots,** peeled and sliced
2 tablespoons	**dried mint leaves**
I	**large tomato,** diced
I cup	**diced cooked ham**
8 cups	**hot cooked rice**
I cup	**minced fresh parsley**

Dice chicken into bite-size pieces, removing visible fat. In a large stockpot, bring chicken, broth and onion to boil and then cover and simmer slowly for 30 minutes. Add carrots and mint leaves and simmer another 20 minutes. Add tomato and ham and simmer 10 minutes more.

Ladle soup into 8 individual shallow serving bowls. Spray a 1-cup size dish or measuring cup with nonstick cooking spray. Press I cup of rice firmly into cup, compacting rice to about $3/4$ cup. Invert pressed rice into center of soup bowl so that mounded rice is sticking up higher than soup. Repeat for each soup bowl. Sprinkle with a little parsley to garnish and serve warm. Makes 8 servings.

CHILEAN RICE (CHILE)

2 tablespoons	**olive oil**
1/4 cup	**chopped onion**
1 teaspoon	**minced garlic**
2 tablespoons	**finely diced red bell peppers**
2 tablespoons	**finely diced carrots**
1 1/2 cups	**uncooked long-grain rice**
2 1/4 cups	**hot chicken broth**
1 teaspoon	**salt**
	cilantro, for garnish

In a large saucepan, heat oil. Stir in onion, garlic, bell pepper and carrots. Saute vegetables for 2–3 minutes. Add rice and stir thoroughly to coat rice in oil. Stir hot chicken broth and salt into rice mixture. Reduce heat to low. Cover and simmer for 15–20 minutes until liquid is completely absorbed into rice. Before serving, fluff rice with a fork. Serve as a side to grilled chicken or steak. Garnish with chopped cilantro, if desired. Makes 4 servings.

PLANTAINS AND RICE (CUBA)

3 tablespoons	**coconut oil**
1	**small onion,** diced
1	**red bell pepper,** diced
3 cloves	**garlic,** minced
1 cup	**uncooked short-grain brown rice**
3 cups	**hot vegetable broth**
2	**medium ripe plantains,** diced
2 cans (14 ounces each)	**black beans,** drained and rinsed
juice and zest of 1	**lime**
1 teaspoon	**cayenne pepper sauce**
1/2 teaspoon	**salt**
1/2 cup	**chopped cilantro,** plus extra for garnish

In a large frying pan, heat oil over medium-high heat; add the onion and saute for 2 minutes. Add the bell pepper and garlic and cook for another 2–3 minutes, until onion and bell pepper are soft and fragrant.

Add rice to the frying pan, stirring until coated in oil. Begin adding the hot broth 1/2 cup at a time, stirring constantly until moisture is absorbed. (You will probably only need to use about 2 cups of broth until the rice is cooked through, but the extra cup is good to have in case you need a little more.) After about half the broth has been added, stir in the plantains and continue the cooking process, stirring in broth in 1/2 cup increments.

Once rice is cooked through, stir in black beans, lime juice and zest, pepper sauce, salt and cilantro, reserving a little extra cilantro for garnish. Makes 4–6 servings.

DESSERTS AND SWEET TREATS

CHOCOLATE CHIP RICE PUDDING

1 1/2 cups	**milk**
1 large box (5.9 ounces)	**chocolate flavored instant pudding mix**
1 container (8 ounces)	**frozen whipped topping,** thawed
1 1/2 cups	**chilled cooked white rice**
1/3 cup	**mini chocolate chips,** divided

In a large bowl, whisk together the milk and pudding mix until pudding thickens. Using a rubber spatula, fold whipped topping into pudding until blended well. Gently fold rice into pudding, breaking up any clumps. Stir all but 1 tablespoon chocolate chips into pudding. Spoon evenly into individual serving bowls and top with remaining chocolate chips. Chill until ready to serve. Makes 6 servings.

CHERRY CHEESECAKE RICE PUDDING

1 1/4 cups	**milk**
1 box (3.4 ounces)	**cheesecake flavored instant pudding mix**
1 container (8 ounces)	**frozen whipped topping,** thawed
2 cups	**chilled cooked white rice**
1 can (20 ounces)	**cherry pie filling**

In a large bowl, whisk together milk and pudding mix until pudding thickens. Using a rubber spatula, fold whipped topping into pudding until blended well. Gently fold rice into pudding, breaking up any clumps. Spoon evenly into individual serving bowls and top with pie filling. Makes 6 servings.

CLASSIC RICE PUDDING

1 1/2 cups	**cooked medium-grain white rice**
2 cups	**milk,** divided
1/4 teaspoon	**salt**
1	**egg,** beaten
1/2 teaspoon	**cinnamon**
1/4 cup	**sugar**
1 tablespoon	**butter or margarine**
1/2 teaspoon	**vanilla extract**

In a large saucepan, combine cooked rice, 1 1/2 cups milk and salt. Over medium heat, cook for 10 minutes stirring occasionally to prevent sticking while pudding thickens. Reduce heat to low and continue to simmer an additional 5 minutes stirring frequently to prevent sticking. Remove from heat.

In a small bowl, whisk together beaten egg, 1/2 cup milk and cinnamon. Stir 2 spoonful's of warm pudding mixture quickly into beaten egg mixture and immediately stir the contents of the bowl into the pudding until thoroughly combined. Cook an additional 2–3 minutes over medium heat, stirring constantly. Remove from heat. Stir in sugar, butter and vanilla. Serve warm or chilled. Makes 4 servings.

Fruit Variation: Stir 2/3 cup dried cranberries or raisins into pudding when you add egg mixture.

CARDAMOM
PISTACHIO RICE PUDDING

³/4 cup	**uncooked basmati rice**
3 cups	**water**
2 cans (14 ounces each)	**regular coconut milk**
	pinch of salt
I teaspoon	**cardamom**
¹/2 cup	**sugar**
I teaspoon	**vanilla extract**
	diced pistachios, for garnish

In a large saucepan, bring to a boil the rice, water, coconut milk and salt. Reduce heat to low and simmer for 30–40 minutes, stirring occasionally, until mixture is thickened to the consistency of oatmeal. Remove from heat and stir in remaining ingredients. Serve chilled, sprinkled with pistachios on top. Makes 4–6 servings.

MANGO STICKY RICE

2 1/4 cups	**uncooked glutinous rice**
1 teaspoon	**vanilla extract**
1/2 cup	**coconut milk**
2	**large ripe mangos,** peeled and diced
4 tablespoons	**sugar,** divided
1 tablespoon	**lime juice**
1 teaspoon	**lime zest**

Rinse rice in a colander until water runs clear. Place in a bowl and pour in enough water to cover rice. Add vanilla. Refrigerate overnight.

Steam rice in a steamer basket* until fully cooked but not mushy, about 45 minutes. The rice should be sticky. Transfer rice to a large serving bowl. Stir in coconut milk. Chill in refrigerator until cold.

Toss mangos with 1 tablespoon of sugar, lime juice and lime zest. Serve by spooning rice into bowls and topping with mango mixture. Makes 4–6 servings.

Note: You can steam the rice in a bamboo steamer or the metal kind of steamer basket that you can place in the bottom of a pan. If the holes in your steamer are too large, line it first with cheesecloth. It is important, for proper texture, that the rice is steamed, not boiled.

OLD FASHIONED BAKED RICE CUSTARD

4	**eggs**
I teaspoon	**salt**
1/2 cup	**sugar**
2 1/2 cups	**whole milk**
I teaspoon	**lemon zest**
2 teaspoons	**vanilla extract**
I teaspoon	**cardamom**
1 1/2 cups	**cooked white rice**
1/2 cup	**raisins**
1/2 cup	**sweetened dried cranberries**
I teaspoon	**cinnamon**
1/2 teaspoon	**nutmeg**

Preheat oven to 325 degrees.

In a medium bowl, whisk together the eggs, salt and sugar. Place milk in a microwave-safe bowl and heat in microwave oven until bubbles begin to form, about 90 seconds. Stirring constantly, slowly pour the hot milk into egg mixture in a small, thin stream. Stir in the lemon zest, vanilla, cardamom, rice, raisins and cranberries.

Butter a 2-quart baking dish. Pour mixture into dish and place dish in a large roasting pan. Pour hot water into roasting pan, filling halfway up the side of the baking dish. Bake for 1 1/2 hours, or until set in center. Chill before serving. Makes 6–8 servings.

PUMPKIN SPICE RICE PUDDING

1 can (12 ounces)	**evaporated milk**
3 cups	**cooked white rice**
1 cup	**canned pumpkin**
$1/2$ cup	**brown sugar**
1 teaspoon	**cinnamon**
$1/8$ teaspoon	**nutmeg**
$1/8$ teaspoon	**ground cloves**
$1/4$ teaspoon	**salt**
	whipped topping, for garnish

In a large saucepan, combine milk, rice, pumpkin, brown sugar, cinnamon, nutmeg, cloves and salt. Cook over medium heat for 9–11 minutes, or until pudding starts to thicken. Spoon rice pudding into a medium serving bowl or into 6–8 individual serving dishes. Garnish with a dollop of whipped topping before serving. Makes 6–8 servings.

TOFFEE
BUTTERSCOTCH RICE PUDDING

1 1/4 cups	**milk**
1 box (3.4 ounces)	**butterscotch flavored instant pudding mix**
1 container (8 ounces)	**frozen whipped topping,** thawed
2 cups	**chilled cooked white rice**
2/3 cup	**Heath Toffee Bits,** divided

In a medium bowl, whisk milk and pudding mix together until it thickens. Using a rubber spatula, fold whipped topping into pudding mixture until well combined. Fold rice into pudding, breaking up any clumps. Reserve 2 tablespoons of toffee bits and stir remaining toffee bits into pudding mixture. Sprinkle reserved toffee bits over top. Makes 6 servings.

DESSERT SUSHI ROLLS

1/2 cup	**uncooked short-grain white rice**
1 can (12 ounces)	**coconut milk**
2 tablespoons	**sugar**
1 cup	**thinly sliced strawberries**
2	**kiwis,** peeled and thinly sliced

In a medium saucepan bring the rice, coconut milk and sugar to a boil. Reduce heat to a simmer and let cook 18–20 minutes, until rice is very tender. Remove from heat and let cool to warm.

On a sheet of plastic wrap, lay slices of strawberries and kiwis in a row overlapping slightly down the center of the plastic wrap. Spoon the rice mixture on top of fruit, making about a 2-inch diameter tube of rice. Wrap plastic wrap over top, forming a tube. Twist ends of plastic wrap to close. Repeat to make 2 12-inch tubes. Refrigerate for 2 hours, or until very cold. Remove plastic wrap and slice into 2-inch pieces. Serve with fruit on top. Makes 12 pieces.

HOT RICE CEREAL WITH MANGO AND PINEAPPLE

1 cup	**uncooked Arborio rice**
2 cups	**water**
2 cups	**milk**
1/3 cup	**sugar**
	pinch of salt
1/4 cup	**minced crystallized ginger**
1/4 teaspoon	**cardamom**
1/2 teaspoon	**cinnamon**
1	**mango,** peeled and diced
1 can (8 ounces)	**pineapple tidbits,** drained

In a large saucepan, boil rice in water for 15 minutes. Rice will be undercooked. Drain any excess water. Add milk, sugar and salt to rice. Bring to a simmer and cook 5 minutes, stirring frequently. Stir in crystallized ginger and spices. Cook another 5 minutes.

Spoon rice into serving bowls and top with mango and pineapple. Makes 6–8 servings.

SOUTH OF THE BORDER HORCHATA

¾ cup	**uncooked white rice**
1 cup	**blanched almonds**
1	**cinnamon stick**
4 cups	**hot water**
½ cup	**sugar**
	pinch of salt
1 cup	**cold water**

Place rice in a blender and blend until rice is in small bits, about 30 seconds.

In a large bowl, stir together the blended rice bits, almonds, cinnamon stick and hot water. Let stand covered on countertop for about 8 hours, stirring every hour or so.

Discard the cinnamon stick. Add sugar and salt. Pour mixture into blender and blend until very smooth, about 90 seconds. Strain through a fine mesh strainer. Stir in cold water. Add in additional cold water if needed to reach a consistency you like. Serve over ice. Makes 4 servings.

NOTES

NOTES

NOTES

NOTES

METRIC CONVERSION CHART

Volume Measurements		Weight Measurements		Temperature Conversion	
U.S.	Metric	U.S.	Metric	Fahrenheit	Celsius
1 teaspoon	5 ml	1/2 ounce	15 g	250	120
1 tablespoon	15 ml	1 ounce	30 g	300	150
1/4 cup	60 ml	3 ounces	90 g	325	160
1/3 cup	75 ml	4 ounces	115 g	350	180
1/2 cup	125 ml	8 ounces	225 g	375	190
2/3 cup	150 ml	12 ounces	350 g	400	200
3/4 cup	175 ml	1 pound	450 g	425	220
1 cup	250 ml	2 1/4 pounds	1 kg	450	230

 Check out these "101" favorites
for more tasty recipes:

Bacon	**Meatballs**
BBQ	**More Cake Mix**
Blender	**More Ramen**
Cake Mix	**More Slow Cooker**
Canned Biscuits	**Pancake Mix**
Canned Soup	**Pickle**
Casserole	**Potato**
Cheese	**Ramen Noodles**
Chicken	**Rotisserie Chicken**
Chocolate	**Salad**
Dutch Oven	**Slow Cooker**
Eggs	**Toaster Oven**
Gelatin	**Tofu**
Grits	**Tortilla**
Ground Beef	**Yogurt**
Mac & Cheese	**Zucchini**

Each 128 pages, $9.99

Available at bookstores or
directly from GIBBS SMITH
1.800.835.4993
www.gibbs-smith.com
101yum.com

ABOUT THE AUTHORS

Donna Kelly is a passionate home cook and recipe developer. She blogs at Apron Strings, the food blog she does with her daughter Anne. She was invited to compete at the 2014 World Food Championship held in Las Vegas, Nevada, and took second place in her category. She is a regular guest cook on Utah morning television show cooking segments and has appeared on Martha Stewart's Sirius radio show, *Everyday Food*. She is the author of nine cookbooks including *French Toast* and *Quesadillas*. Donna has been an attorney for more than 32 years, mostly as a prosecutor handling sex crimes, domestic violence and child abuse cases. She is a mom to five adult children and lives in Utah with her husband of 37 years.

Stephanie Ashcraft was raised in Indiana. She received a bachelor's degree in family science and a teaching certificate from Brigham Young University. Stephanie loves teaching, interacting with people, and spending time with friends and family. Stephanie has taught hundreds of classes and appeared on hundreds of television and news programs all over the country sharing ways that families can save time and money in the kitchen. Stephanie and her husband, Ivan, reside in Salem, Utah, with their five children.